Editor
Mary Kaye Taggart

Editorial Manager
Karen J. Goldfluss, M.S. Ed.

Editor-in-Chief
Sharon Coan, M.S. Ed.

Illustrators
Bruce Hedges
Barb Lorseyedi

Interior Art Design
Michelle M. McAuliffe
Marsha W. Black

Cover Artist
Denise Bauer

Art Coordinator
Cheri Macoubrie Wilson

Creative Director
Elayne Roberts

Imaging
James Edward Grace

Product Manager
Phil Garcia

Publishers
Rachelle Cracchiolo, M.S. Ed.
Mary Dupuy Smith, M.S. Ed.

BUSY TEACHER'S GUIDE
ART LESSONS

Authors

Michelle M. McAuliffe

Marsha W. Black

Teacher Created Materials, Inc.
6421 Industry Way
Westminster, CA 92683
www.teachercreated.com

ISBN-1-57690-471-7

©1999 Teacher Created Materials, Inc.
Reprinted, 2003
Made in U.S.A.

Table of Contents

Introduction
  How to Use This Book 4

Lessons
  1. **Wheel and Deal in Color**
     Color Mixing 6

  2. **Noteworthy Neutrals**
     Using Neutrals 8

  3. **Art Shape-Up**
     Basic Shapes 10

  4. **Crafty, Curvaceous Contours**
     Line 12

  5. **Ad-Fad**
     Value of Dark and Light 14

  6. **Tackling Texture**
     Texture Techniques 16

  7. **Kaleidoscope Cutup**
     Spatial Relationships 18

  8. **Exploring the Sun and Shadows**
     Contrast 20

  9. **Dangerous Dragons, Terrible Trolls, and Weird Wombats**
     Organizing the Elements of Art 22

  10. **Practicing Perspective**
      Perspective 24

  11. **Toucan Mosaics**
      Asymmetrical Balance 26

  12. **Royal Foil Masks**
      Dominance 28

  13. **Personality Photo**
      Expression 30

  14. **Rectangle Riot**
      Negative Space 32

  15. **Liquefaction Action**
      Proportion 34

  16. **Sun Catchers**
      Organizing the Elements of Art 36

  17. **Mag Pix**
      Focal Point 38

  18. **Stained Glass Pizzazz**
      Repetition and Overlapping 40

Table of Contents *(cont.)*

19. **Lots of Polka Dots**
    Symmetrical and Asymmetrical Balance 42

20. **Scratch a Batch of Art**
    Unity, Harmony, and Variety 44

21. **Print and Pattern**
    Figure-to-Ground Relationships 46

22. **Design a No-Picture Picture**
    Abstract Art. 48

23. **Mosaic Mania**
    Mosaic Technique 50

24. **Positive and Negative Design**
    Forms and Negative Space 52

25. **Print Pix**
    Printing Techniques. 54

26. **Kite Flight**
    Collage 56

27. **Wriggle into Weaving**
    Weaving Techniques 58

28. **Dynamic Dimensions**
    Three-Dimensional Art 60

29. **Name Game**
    Graphic Technique 62

30. **Seed-sational Creations**
    Interdisciplinary Art 64

31. **Weather Art**
    Multifaceted Compositions 66

32. **Presents for Parents** 68

33. **Let's Talk Turkey** 70

34. **Awesome Ornaments** 72

35. **Voilà! Valentines!** 74

36. **Bright Bunnies and Egg-cellent Eggs** 76

Management

Art Lesson—Generic Form 78

Art Sources 80

Introduction

Elementary art education exists as an important developmental tool for the nurturing of creative and academic skills in young children. It helps in the process of sharpening the senses and aids in developing eye-hand coordination. It contributes significantly to small muscle control. Art assists in maturing the mind and emotions of the child through its educational and formative qualities.

The importance of art as an element in educational curriculums cannot be overstated. Children have a basic need to express themselves by making things. Color and form offer the child opportunities for creative responses to awaken dormant images within the imagination and assist in bringing these images into tangible reality.

Ideas must be converted into visual language by the child with the teacher acting as a guide in an accepting environment. The teacher can accomplish this through suggestion and encouragement while allowing the child to work freely and without undue interference. This will give the child a sense of accomplishment and joy.

Art is a civilizing and cultural influence. Children should be taught to appreciate art during their formative years. The authors created this book to help teachers nurture and bring to fruition the child's creative talents.

How to Use This Book

Busy Teacher's Guide: Art Lessons is designed to make the teaching of art an easy and enjoyable experience for all teachers. The projects in this book have been tested thoroughly, first by the authors and then in the classroom. Testing assures the instructor that the finished projects will be functional and attractive.

The teacher who selects this book as an art text will have more than enough projects for the entire school year. Students will learn the basic elements of art and how to apply them. Some lessons are designed to help sharpen their drawing skills, while others will introduce a variety of techniques and materials. Also, holiday projects are included which the teacher can use to decorate the classroom or send home with the students.

Many states now have proficiency standards for art; the lessons in this book will meet many of these requirements. Teachers will find it easy to choose specific skills to strengthen their students' weak points. The lessons can be simplified or made more complex, depending on the backgrounds of the students involved.

The art experiences students receive when applying a variety of techniques and working with many different materials increase their competency in the theory and practice of art. The students will also add new terms (which are informally introduced in the lessons) to their art vocabularies.

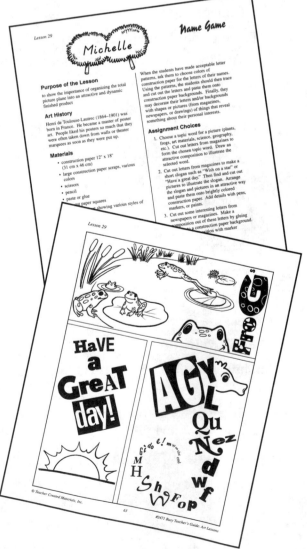

Introduction *(cont.)*

How to Use This Book *(cont.)*

This book is designed to meet the needs of busy teachers. Each lesson has a "Purpose" ready to be copied into a lesson plan book. Each lesson also has an "Art History" section which describes a famous artist and artwork. It would be beneficial to show these famous artworks to the students and discuss them. (Some sources for the art are listed on page 80.) The materials needed for one student to complete the main project are listed in the "Materials" section. Any additional materials needed to complete the "Assignment Choices" are listed under the subheading "Variations." The listed materials are readily available and reasonably priced. Many may be recycled from everyday items. The "Procedure" section of each lesson is written to the teacher, and it gives the directions for the main art project. The "Assignment Choices" section is student-directed, and it gives the students one or more variations on the main project from which to choose. The "Connection" section points out a link between the artist highlighted in the "Art History" section and the lesson. Finally, on the page following each lesson, patterns for and/or illustrations of the finished work are provided to help the teacher visualize the completed work. In addition to the prepared lessons, you will find a generic form on pages 78 and 79 which may be used to create your own lessons.

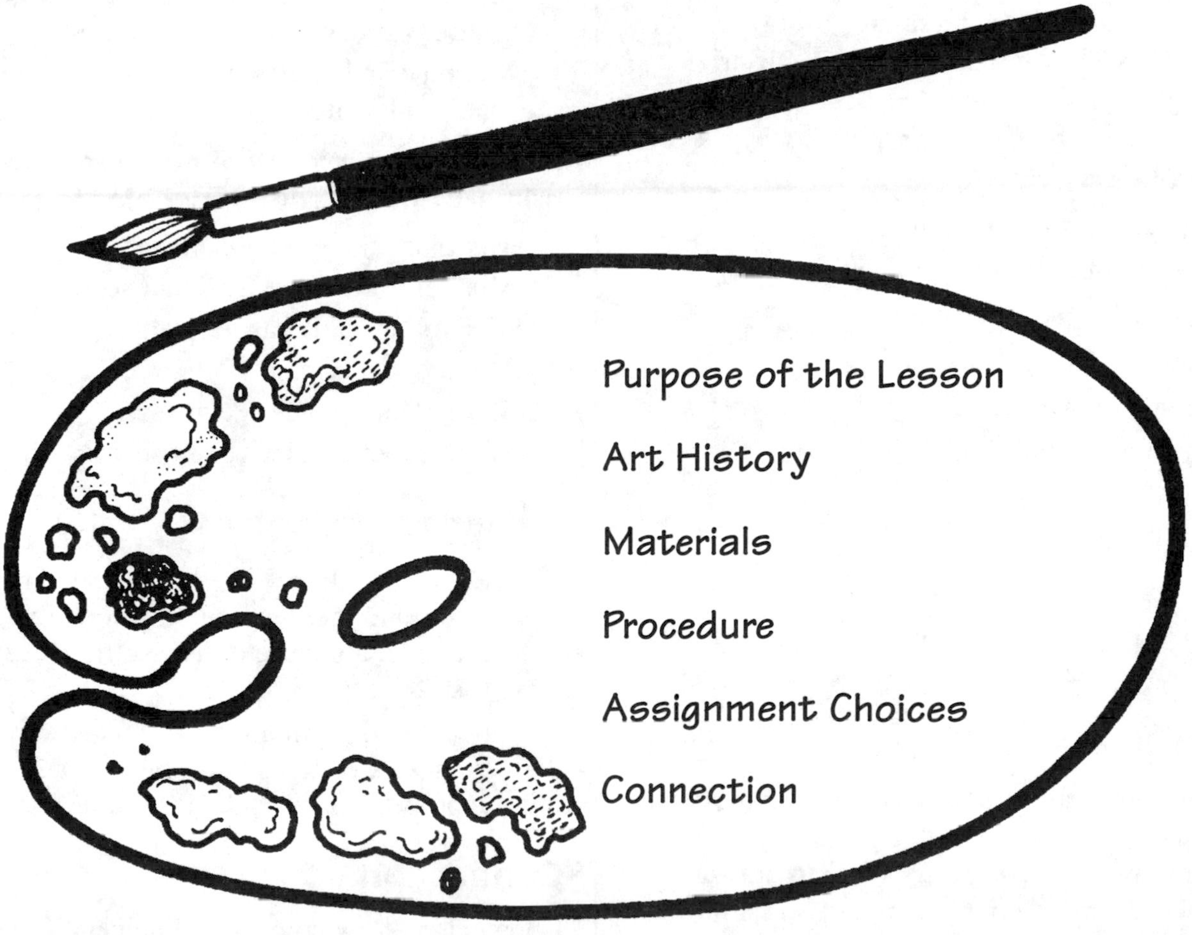

Purpose of the Lesson

Art History

Materials

Procedure

Assignment Choices

Connection

Gentle, constructive criticism of finished or in-progress work will help the growth of an elementary student's skill level. Criticism, however, should always be accompanied by compliments about what is good in the individual student's work. A pupil's enthusiasm and hard work are the mark of a competent teacher.

Wheel and Deal in Color

Purpose of the Lesson

to acquaint the students with unmixed primary colors (red, yellow, blue), mixed secondary colors (green, orange, violet), and intermediate colors (red-violet, blue-violet, yellow-green, blue-green, yellow-orange, and red-orange)

Art History

Sonia Terk Delaunay (1885–1980). Born in Russia, she was influenced by Orphic Cubism. She used many multicolored arcs to form intricate circles in her composition "Electric Prisms."

Materials

- white construction paper
- black, thin-line, felt-tip pen
- black ballpoint pen
- ruler
- compass with pencil
- tempera paint
- mixing tray
- water
- brush
- pictures of objects with large, round areas (horn, tractor, drum, wreath, etc.)

Procedure

Have the students draw objects with large, round areas such as a vehicle with a large wheel or a child's swimming pool. Ask them to draw a color wheel with a compass and divide it into 12 equal parts. Tell the students to number the sections outside of the circle.

Primary colors cannot be created by mixing other colors.

Paint section 1 pure blue.
Paint section 5 pure yellow.
Paint section 9 pure red.

Secondary colors are made by mixing two primary colors together.

Mix yellow and blue to make green. Paint section 3 green.

Mix yellow and red to make orange. Paint section 7 orange.

Mix blue and red to make violet. Paint section 11 violet.

Intermediate colors are made by mixing a primary and a secondary color together.

Mix blue and green. Paint section 2.
Mix yellow and green. Paint section 4.
Mix yellow and orange. Paint section 6.
Mix red and orange. Paint section 8.
Mix red and violet. Paint section 10.
Mix blue and violet. Paint section 12.

Assignment Choices

1. Create a picture which shows overlapping forms and their combined colors, for example, a picture of leaves, flowers, and a vase.

2. Use colors from all three classes of colors to make a composition. Include an appropriate background for your picture.

Connection

Knowledge of the color wheel helped Sonia Terk Delaunay make a famous painting. Color mixing in this lesson will apply to the art pieces the students make in the future.

6

Noteworthy Neutrals

Purpose of the Lesson

to introduce the students to the neutrals white, black, and gray and to show their relationship to the colors of the spectrum

Note to the Teacher

Neutrals differ from the colors on the color wheel in the quantity of light that they reflect. Black reflects no color at all. It absorbs the colors of the spectrum equally. White reflects all colors (or wavelengths of light) equally. Shades of gray reflect some light and absorb some light, depending on the darkness or lightness of the shade. This is why neutrals enhance all colors. Consider this principle when selecting background or framing materials.

Art History

Louise Nevelson (1900–1988) was born in Kiev, Russia. Her compositions were usually done in neutrals, white and black. However, sometimes she used gold for whole works or for accent. Her sculpture "Mirror Shadow II" is flat black with white and gold accents.

Materials

- black, white, and gray construction paper
- black marker
- eraser
- fine-line, black pen
- scissors
- pencil
- paste or glue
- scrap white paper (may be used on one side)
- superhold hairspray

Procedure

Ask each student to draw several sketches (on scrap paper) of nature scenes of their choice. Remind them that they only have black, gray, and white to work with. (They may have shades of neutrals also.) First, each student must choose a background neutral and use the remaining neutrals to complete his or her picture. The students cut out forms from the construction paper and then paste them on their backgrounds. The forms may also be added with marker or black ink pen.

Assignment Choices

1. On 9" x 12" (23 cm x 31 cm) gray construction paper, draw a seascape. Make a small pattern of a duck, gull, or other bird. Using this pattern, cut four or more birds from black construction paper and the same number from white construction paper. Paste each group on the paper so that the birds are flying in opposite directions. Add clouds and the sun.

2. Start with a piece of light blue 12" x 18" (31 cm x 46 cm) construction paper. With a pencil lightly sketch a winter scene of your choice: snowmobiling, skating, skiing, tobogganing, etc. When the sketch is finished and checked by the teacher, color it in with white, gray, and black chalk. (Many interesting textures can be achieved by rubbing, erasing, etc.) When your picture is finished, spray it with superhold hairspray to fix the chalk permanently.

Connection

As students explore neutrals in this lesson, they can enjoy the discipline of working with white, gray, and black as Louise Nevelson did.

Purpose of the Lesson

to teach the students that all representational drawing consists of a variety of two- and three-dimensional basic shapes (Some basic shapes are circle, oval, square, rectangle, diamond, pyramid, triangle, and cylinder. Variations of some of these shapes can be found in many drawings.)

Art History

Henri Matisse (1869–1954) was born in France. He used bright colors and many shapes in his compositions. He said he was "drawing with scissors." In "Beasts of the Sea" he gives us the colors, shapes, and feeling of deep-sea life.

Materials

- old magazines
- ruler
- compass
- protractor
- paper or light cardboard
- scissors
- 9" x 12" (23 cm x 31 cm) white construction paper
- scrap construction paper, any colors
- paste or glue
- markers
- black ballpoint pen

Variations

- dowel
- string
- paper fringe for banner
- star patterns (different sizes)
- old seed catalogs

Procedure

Ask each student to tear an interesting picture from an old magazine. Tell them to search for and circle as many basic shapes as they can find in the pictures.

Have the students choose four or more geometric shapes to make interesting designs. Remind them that geometric shapes must be uniform and accurate. An easy way to have uniform shapes is to cut one shape of each type from light cardboard and trace the shapes on the composition from the pattern.

Signs, murals, wall hangings, etc., lend themselves to this type of project. Encourage your students to use their imaginations and lots of color!

Assignment Choices

1. Design a banner, quilt, flag, or other patriotic emblem, using the colors red, white, and blue.
2. Draw a crazy quilt, using a variety of colors and textures.
3. Design a race car from random geometric shapes.
4. Find clippings of flowers or plants from seed catalogs or old magazines. Cut out pictures in rectangles or squares of uniform size. Combine them with plain construction-paper shapes to make an interesting composition.

Connection

The works of Henri Matisse teach students to use color and shape to create a mood when composing pictures with abstract forms.

Crafty, Curvaceous Contours

Purpose of the Lesson

to show students that line defines the shape of things and that it is an important element of art

Art History

Vincent van Gogh (1853–1890) was born in France, and he loved art. In his short lifetime, he completed 750 paintings and 1,600 drawings. Many of his paintings give a feeling of movement. One of his last paintings was "Starry Night," which gives a feeling of stars pulsating in the night sky.

Materials

- colored construction paper
- white construction paper
- paste or glue
- ballpoint pen or pencil
- markers
- scissors

Variations

- string or thread
- crayons
- brown paper bags

Procedure

Have the students choose themes for their compositions. Some ideas are musical instruments, sports, art, school functions, and holidays.

Ask the students to draw objects for their pictures using continuous lines. Explain that the challenge of this activity is that the pen or pencil should not be lifted from the page until the drawing is completed. This requires discipline and concentration!

Next, ask the students to cut out the drawings, being sure to leave all of the lines intact. They may then arrange their drawings on construction paper to make pleasing compositions. Several colors of construction paper may be used in the background.

Assignment Choices

1. Make contour drawings with a marker on brightly colored construction paper. Cut the entire drawing out in an interesting shape. Paste the shape on a neutral background.

2. Use a piece of string (or heavy thread) dipped in glue to make a contour design on construction paper. After it has dried, cut out the design and paste it on an appropriate background.

3. Use a crayon to make a contour drawing on a brown paper bag. The inside of a grocery bag makes a good surface for crayon drawings. Cut out and mount your drawing on brown or black construction paper.

Connection

A study of Vincent van Gogh's fluid lines will create a mood for circular movement as the students make continuous-line drawings.

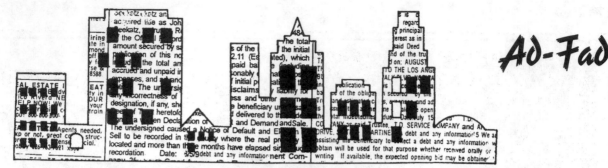

Ad-Fad

Purpose of the Lesson

to show the students the value of the relationship of light and dark tones within the picture plane

Art History

Michelangelo Merisi da Caravaggio (1573–1610) was born in Italy. While still in his twenties, he became a skilled and innovative painter. His use of light and dark shades is masterful. An example of his technical ability in the use of light and shade is seen in "The Calling of St. Matthew."

Materials

- black construction paper
- pencil
- scissors
- paste or glue
- black or red marker (Crayon or paint may be substituted.)
- newspaper want ads

Variations

- comics section of the newspaper
- assorted colored markers
- white construction paper
- red construction paper
- bits of colored tissue paper, string, glitter, etc.

Procedure

Using newspaper want ads, the students cut out shapes of buildings, trees, or any other theme they choose. Lay the newspaper cutouts loosely on black construction paper. Have them move the forms around until a pleasing composition is achieved. Ask the students to paste the forms onto their construction paper backgrounds. They may add details with black markers. For variety, some students may want to use red markers. This is very effective with the black and white.

Assignment Choices

1. Cut out shapes from black construction paper. Paste the forms on a newspaper background. Choose brightly colored markers to add details to the background.

2. Cut out a background from darkly colored newspaper ads. Choose a theme and cut out theme-related shapes from white construction paper. Add accents with black or colored markers to the white forms.

3. Create three-dimensional forms cut out of the colored comics section of the newspaper. For example, you might create a park scene in which butterflies have moving wings, trees have colorful leaves, swings are made with real string for the chains, etc. Mount the forms on a piece of red construction paper. Add glitter for accent or as rays of sunshine.

Connection

Evaluate the artist's use of light and dark tones and apply this principle when working in this lesson with light and dark newspaper copy.

Purpose of the Lesson

to show the students that texture is the actual or visual feeling of a variety of surfaces arranged on a picture plane

Art History

Jan van Eyck (1390–1441) was probably born in Maaseik (now in Belgium). Jan was a court painter known for his skill in painting textures and detail. The painting "Giovanni Arnolfini and His Wife" shows realistic fur, fabric, fire, wood, mirror surface, and many other textures.

Materials

- typing paper or tissue paper
- construction paper
- interesting examples of texture (e.g., wallpaper, sandpaper, burlap)
- crayons
- "found" textures (see below)
- paste or glue
- scissors
- markers
- pencil

Variations

- colored chalk
- superhold hairspray

Procedure

Bring some examples of texture to class for the students to use. Sandpaper, burlap, pennies, paper clips, lace, wallpaper, combs, or anything else with a raised surface would be helpful for this project. Ask the students to find other textures around the classroom.

Show the students how to print these "found" textures by putting a piece of white paper over the texture and coloring over it with a crayon. From their texture print pieces, the students cut out shapes and paste them on a construction paper background. They may enhance their works with crayon lines, glitter, ink, and/or marker.

Assignment Choices

1. Use thin white paper (typing or tissue) and lay it over a texture. Rub over the paper with brightly colored chalk. Spray the print lightly with superhold hairspray. This will fix the chalk permanently. Use these chalk texture rubbings to make a drawing.

2. Cut out designs from thin cardboard or tagboard. Paste these designs onto a construction paper background. Lay a thin piece of construction, tissue, or typing paper on top of the design. Color heavily on the top sheet to make the design appear. Add marker accents. Crop your work to a desired size and frame it.

3. Look for interesting textures in old wallpaper books. Cut out shapes and paste them on a background. Add unifying lines or accents, if needed.

Connection

A variety of textures makes an interesting composition. When the students plan to create future projects, be sure that they add texture to their works.

Kaleidoscope Cutup

Purpose of the Lesson

to show the students that spatial relationship is the placement of forms to create spatial tension within the picture plane

Art History

Frank Stella (1936–   ) was born in Massachusetts, and he studied at Princeton University. His exploration of color, space, and geometric forms has helped create innovative compositions such as "Singerli Variation IV."

Materials

- scissors
- pencil
- ruler
- paste or glue
- construction paper 8 ½" x 11" (22 cm x 28 cm)
- scraps of colored construction paper

Variations

- white construction paper
- black construction paper
- paper punch (notebook-sized holes)

Procedure

Ask the students to cut scraps of colored construction paper into geometric shapes. The figures should be drawn carefully on the paper before being cut out.

Have the students arrange their shapes loosely on construction paper backgrounds. Tell them to check their compositions to see that both the shape and color combinations are attractive. They may want to lightly trace the shapes before they glue them in place so that the pieces get glued exactly as planned. The shapes then may

be glued down carefully so that the sharp points and ends are attached.

Assignment Choices

1. Instead of colored paper, try an arrangement of black forms on a white background or white forms on a black background.

2. Draw a large circle and divide it into six or more equal sections. Using geometric shapes of many colors, make a design in one section. Repeat the same design in the remaining sections so that the design is symmetrical.

3. Punch out holes in several sheets of construction paper, with a paper punch. Divide a large circle into six or more parts and arrange the dots that you have punched out in a symmetrical pattern. Each of the sections should have an identical symmetrical design.

Connection

Students exploring kaleidoscope designs should give as much attention to negative space as they do to the geometric forms.

Exploring the Sun and Shadows

Purpose of the Lesson

to show that form is the use and organization of the elements of art and that contrast enhances the picture plane

Art History

Fritz Scholder (1937–   ) was born in Minnesota and educated in South Dakota, California, Arizona, and New Mexico. His lithograph "Indian Portrait with Tomahawk" is an example of good form because all of its parts work together in unity.

Materials

- black and white construction paper
- scissors
- paste or glue
- crayons or paint
- pencil
- scrap paper for patterns
- glitter, foil, shiny paper, ribbon, colored tissue, etc. (optional)

Variations

- electric iron and ironing surface
- paper towels or newspaper
- window glass or plastic
- black paint and a container
- brush
- glycerin or liquid soap
- colored tissue paper

Procedure

Have the students each decide on a theme for their compositions. Tell them to make patterns for their themes on scrap paper and then cut out the forms from black construction paper. Next, the forms should be laid on white paper backgrounds and traced where they will be pasted. However, the forms should not be pasted down yet but set aside.

Ask the students to then color their backgrounds in bright sunset colors, being careful not to color where the black paper will be pasted. Glitter, foil, shiny paper, or ribbon in thin strips may be added (if desired). When the backgrounds are finished, the black paper forms can be pasted on to complete the pictures.

Assignment Choices

1. Colored tissue paper can be brushed on with thinned white glue instead of the crayon or paint background.

2. For an unusual textural effect, color the background heavily with crayon and iron it between layers of paper towel or newspaper with a warm iron.

3. Using tissue paper and a shiny texture, make a sunset. Paste it behind a piece of glass. Using black paint with a few drops of glycerin or liquid soap added, paint a black silhouette on the front of the glass.

Connection

Repeating colors, shapes, textures, and values in a composition, as Fritz Scholder did, makes a pleasing picture.

Lesson 8

Dangerous Dragons, Terrible Trolls, and Weird Wombats

Purpose of the Lesson

to show the students that total composition is the process of organizing all of the elements of art into a unified whole

Art History

Raffaello Sanzio (1483–1520) was born in Italy. His famous painting "St. George and the Dragon" was painted in 1506 for a duke from his hometown, who wanted to present it to King Henry VII of England.

Materials

- construction paper
- pencil
- paste or glue
- scissors
- markers
- dried grasses or foliage

Variations

- old magazines
- bits of furry material
- transparent or translucent material for wings, such as kitchen plastic wrap, waxed paper, etc.

Procedure

Show the students pictures of dragons, trolls, and wombats (there are examples on page 23). Explain to the students that they are completing a total composition, incorporating line, color, shape, texture, shading, and design. Point out that the drawings are meant to be funny. Ask them to inject a sense of humor into their drawings. They may even invent their own special animals. Dried grasses, foliage, and small brush cuttings will add interest and texture to their compositions.

Assignment Choices

1. Cut out parts of animals from old magazines to create your own weird animal. Explain by saying, "What if an alligator had the head of an elephant and the tail of a lion?" or "What if a monkey had a zebra's body with a giraffe's legs?" Paste the new animals on construction paper and add details with crayon or marker. Write the name of your creature somewhere on the background.

2. Use texture to make furry animals and bright colors to add interest. Your animal could have furry eyebrows, rough horns, or gossamer wings.

3. Invent your own zoo of several imaginary animals. Draw interesting habitats where your animals would be found.

Connection

Raffaello Sanzio's dragon is fierce looking and very frightening. The students, however, should try to make their dragons lighthearted and friendly.

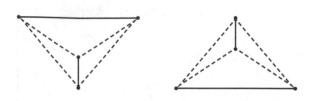 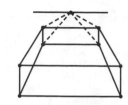

Practicing Perspective

Purpose of the Lesson

to help the students learn to draw in perspective by making compositions that seem to have three dimensions on two-dimensional planes

Art History

Giorgio de Chirico (1888–1978) worked with angular lines, light and shadow, and formalized perspectives in works such as "Mystery & Melancholy of a Street." His paintings have a dreamlike quality. He included strange elements that do not seem to have logical reasons for being in his paintings.

Materials

- 9" x 12"
  (23 cm x 31 cm)
  white drawing
  paper
- pencil

- eraser
- ruler
- black ink pen
- scrap paper

Procedure

Draw an example on the board to show the students two vanishing points. First, draw a straight horizon line. From the ends of the horizon, draw two lines toward a point in the center and below the horizon line. (**Note:** These lines can be drawn above the horizon line as well.) When finished, it should look like two triangles with a common center line. Perspective is a process which causes the observer to think that forms drawn on a two-dimensional plane have three dimensions (length, width, and height). This is done by establishing a vanishing point to fool the eye. When a person looks at forms in the distance, they seem to get smaller.

Ask the students to draw their own medieval castles. Remind them that windows, doors, and other forms must follow the line of the building and get smaller towards the back of the building.

Assignment Choices

1. Draw a block or cube. Erase the lines at the back of the cube. On scrap paper, practice drawing several cubes, erasing the lines at the back of each cube and then shading it to give it thickness and solidity. Try leaving the top plain and shading the sides. Try other shading ideas. When you have found a cube idea that you like, enlarge it and make sure that the sides are accurate. Draw and shade it with a black ink pen.

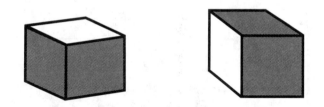

2. Draw a road with a vanishing point. Add trees on both sides of the road. Add other figures of your own choice to make the picture more interesting. Remember to draw the trees smaller and smaller as they approach the horizon line.

3. Another method of achieving perspective is by overlapping forms. An easy way to get an accurate picture is to draw in all of the forms in pencil first and then erase the lines that go behind other forms. When the picture is complete and in proportion, draw and shade it with black ink pen.

Connection

Giorgio de Chirico's masterful command of perspective demonstrates how the illusion of three-dimensional space can be achieved on a two-dimensional plane.

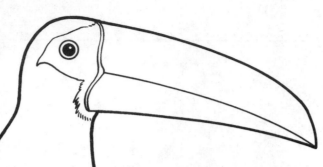

Toucan Mosaics

Purpose of the Lesson

to demonstrate spatial relationships using asymmetrical balance and to introduce a new texture

Art History

Gioacchino Barberi (1783–1857) was born in Rome, Italy. He created miniature mosaics with dark backgrounds. A charming composition is his "Plaque with Parrot Driving Two Turtles," which measures just 2 ³/₄" x 1 ³/₄" (7 cm x 4.5 cm).

Materials

- construction paper
- cardboard
- paste or glue
- eggshells

- permanent marker
- clear gloss
- pencil

Variations

- milk jugs or plastic lids
- old magazines
- burlap
- crayon

- felt
- dowels or thin sticks
- yarn
- fabric glue

Procedure

Ask each student to glue a backing of stiff cardboard onto a piece of 9" x 12" (23 cm x 31 cm) construction paper. They may then use pencils to sketch pictures of toucans (or other designs) onto the backgrounds. Set the backgrounds aside.

Help the students clean eggshells in warm soapy water and remove the membranes. Next, the students should break the shells into small pieces and glue them onto the largest parts of their pictures. The pieces can then be colored with markers. After all of the larger areas are filled in, the details may also be filled in with eggshells.

When the mosaics have dried, spray them with gloss.

Note: In this project it is important to let a little of the background show through around each piece that is glued to the picture.

Assignment Choices

1. Glue a cardboard backing onto a piece of 9" x 12" (23 cm x 31 cm) construction paper. Sketch a picture or design onto the background in pencil. Instead of eggshells, substitute bits of plastic from lids or milk jugs. Color the mosaic pieces with marker. Spray them with gloss.

2. Draw a picture on construction paper. Look for texture pieces in magazines (ads for carpet, towels, draperies, etc.). Tear or cut the magazine pictures into small bits. Paste the pieces onto your picture. Spray the mosaic with gloss.

3. Draw a picture with black crayon onto burlap. Cut out small felt pieces and glue them onto the crayoned drawing. Outline the felt pieces with yarn pieces that have been glued on. Fold down the top of the burlap, stitch, and insert a dowel. Use the mosaic as a wall hanging.

Connection

As the students explore the use of a variety of materials to make mosaics, remind them that Gioacchino Barberi also used different materials in his mosaics. Perhaps the students can invent their own miniature mosaics as Barberi did.

Royal Foil Masks

Purpose of the Lesson

to explain how to give a work of art a dominant point of interest and ways of painting on foil

Art History

Lois Mailou Jones (1905–   ) was born in Boston. She taught at Howard University for 47 years. Her composition "Les Fetiches" is a grouping of masks with an African influence.

Materials

- foil (Heavy duty foil is best.)
- pencil with a medium-sharp point
- cardboard
- tempera paints
- dishwashing soap or glycerin
- paintbrush
- construction paper
- paste or glue
- paper and pencil for planning
- markers

Procedure

This project is excellent to use when studying ethnic groups. For example, have the students sketch Chinese mask ideas on scrap paper. When the sketches are finished, tell the students to each wrap a piece of foil over a piece of cardboard and then place the sketch on top of the foil. The students should then trace over their drawings with medium-sharp pencils. When the sketches are removed, the designs should remain on the foil.

Next, have the students paint their foil designs, using a few drops of dishwashing soap or glycerin in paint. (The soap will help the paint adhere to the foil.) When dry, the foil designs can be mounted on construction paper. Chinese motifs (which can be found in an encyclopedia) should be added along the edges of the construction paper.

Assignment Choices

1. Draw and paint an Egyptian figure such as King Tutankhamen on foil. Mount the figure on gold construction paper. Add small drawings of pyramids, the Sphinx, or other Egypt-related objects around the paper.
2. Draw and paint a Mexican mask and mount it on a colorful background. Add such things as guitars, maracas, haciendas, and a sombrero to the background.

Connection

Just as Lois Mailou Jones has done, the students will also enhance and broaden their art ideas by studying masks from many cultures.

Personality Photo

Purpose of the Lesson

to show that expression is the integration of elements in order to express a concept, emotion, or mood

Art History

Audrey Flack (1931–   ) has been a New Yorker all of her life. She is a photorealist, and her painting entitled "Marilyn" is a visual commentary on the life of Marilyn Monroe. She arranged the elements of the picture to make an attractive and colorful composition.

Materials

- 12" x 18" (31 cm x 46 cm) white construction paper
- old magazines
- scissors
- paste or glue
- colored chalk, crayons, or markers

Note: If chalk is used, an inexpensive can of superhold hairspray will act as a fixative on the chalked areas.

Procedure

Ask the students to think about themselves, their likes, dislikes, talents, and what makes them unique. Tell them to cut out pictures that represent some of these things from old magazines. For example, a student who is an animal lover might cut out pictures of cats, dogs, and other animals. Allow the students to also cut out words that apply to them.

When the students have found their collections of words and pictures that represent their personalities, the cutouts should be pasted onto white construction paper backgrounds. Unifying details may be added to these personality "photos," using markers, crayons, or colored chalk.

Assignment Choices

1. Make a personality "photo" of your pet or a pet you would like to own. Cut out magazine pictures of special foods your pet likes and find pictures of special things that your pet likes to do (such as taking walks or playing with toys).

2. Make a personality "photo" of your favorite character from a story, book, or comic strip that you have read. What makes the character special? Find pictures and words to represent those special things and make a composition.

Connection

Audrey Flack included many facets of Marilyn Monroe's life, along with her own ideas, to make a personality statement. From this artist we learn that careful planning before a composition is started makes the difference between a mediocre or a quality picture.

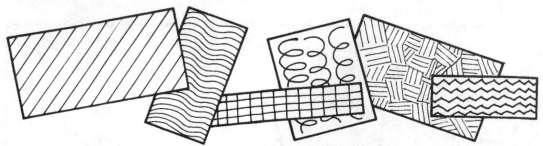

Rectangle Riot

Purpose of the Lesson

to show that the negative space of a flat surface on which the artist imposes an idea is a two-dimensional picture plane

Art History

Salvador Dali (1904–1989) was born in Spain. He used his imagination to create strange forms that seemed almost real. He invented elephants with bird legs, giraffes with flaming necks, melting watches, and other surreal images. "The Elephants" is one of the works that made him famous.

Materials

- white construction paper
- pencil
- markers or crayons
- scrap paper for planning

Variations

- paste or glue
- ruler
- magazines or catalogs
- scissors
- collection of colored, textured papers

Procedure

Ask each student to draw five to six rectangles on a piece of white paper. The rectangles should vary in size and proportion. Challenge the students to choose a single, unifying theme for the pictures they are about to draw. Some theme ideas might be zoo, circus, flowers, cartoon characters, and airplanes. This is not an easy project, and the students may need suggestions and supervision.

The students will be drawing within the rectangles pictures which represent their chosen themes. Planning on scrap paper first might be helpful to the students. They should try to think of ways to draw all of the pictures into the basic theme to unify and give importance to the total composition of the picture.

Assignment Choices

1. Make a collage by using magazine or catalog pictures. Paste the pictures in the rectangles. Unify the theme by drawing or pasting cutouts between and around the pictures.

2. Draw the story of your life (starting at birth) in the rectangles. Draw the hospital where you were born, the school where you attended kindergarten, a picture of your family, a favorite vacation or sport, and a picture of your current home. Finish the composition with an interesting title.

3. Make an abstract design in each rectangle, using a variety of interesting papers. Construction paper, foil, gift wrap, wallpaper, fuzzy velour paper, and others may be used. Using many textures will enhance your abstract composition. Include an eye-catching title.

Connection

Salvador Dali was a fine technical draftsman. His examples of careful drawing and attention to detail should inspire students to imitate his technical ability.

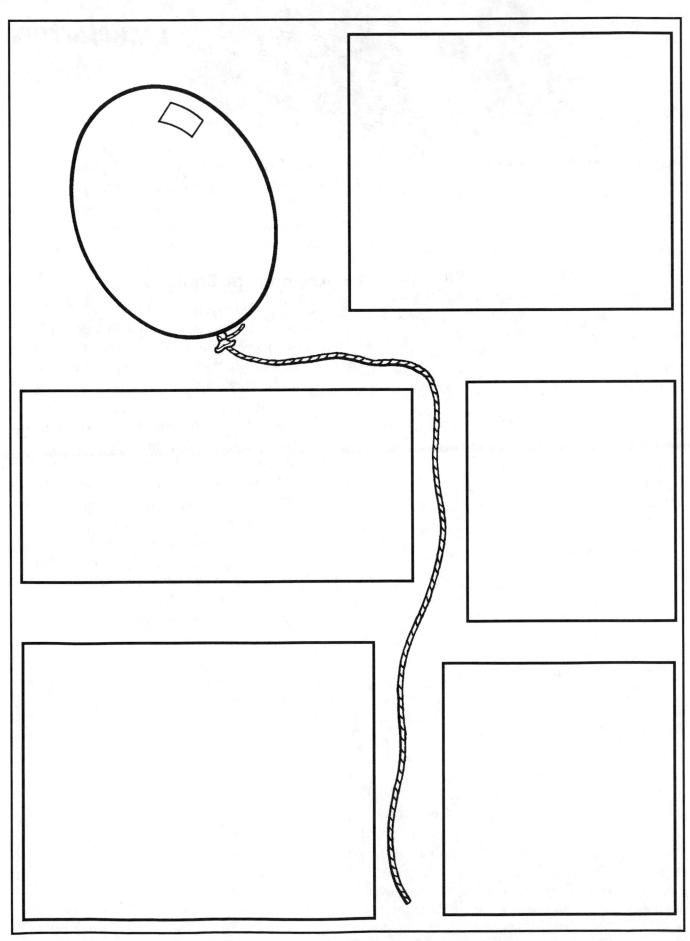

Liquefaction Action

Purpose of the Lesson

to demonstrate that in a picture proportion is very important

Art History

Many of Claude Monet's (1840–1926) paintings were outdoor scenes. He used a special brush technique in which he layered small patches of color. In his painting entitled "The River," Monet flooded his landscape with sunlight.

Materials

- large construction paper
- watercolors
- 1" (2.54 cm) paintbrush
- scissors
- pencil
- crayon chips
- paper towels
- crayons
- electric iron

Variations

- blue dye
- cotton material scraps
- markers

Procedure

Ask the students to draw trees, beginning with the trunks, then adding smaller branches, and finally branching off into twigs. Next, have them use crayons to color in the tree branches, trunks, flowers, and grass.

Let the students sprinkle brightly colored crayon chips on the branches for leaves. Carefully place a paper towel over the crayon chips and iron over the paper towel with a warm iron, melting the

chips. Large areas of color will appear.

Instruct the students to paint over their compositions with pale blue watercolor, creating a crayon resist. Once the pictures have dried, they may be framed with construction paper.

Assignment Choices

1. Sprinkle crayon chips on construction paper, place a paper towel on top, and iron with a warm iron. Make a picture or design with black marker to create interesting detail.

2. Peel the paper label from a crayon. Cut notches along the side of the crayon. Draw with the side of the crayon to create an abstract design. Place a paper towel over the design and press it with a warm iron.

3. Heavily color a design onto a square scrap of cotton material with crayons. Press the scrap with a warm iron. Crinkle the material piece into a ball. Smooth it out, dip it in dye, and let it dry. Iron the scrap again with a warm iron. The product may be used for a wall hanging.

Connection

A study of Claude Monet's trees and his use of color will inspire the students to create meaningful landscapes.

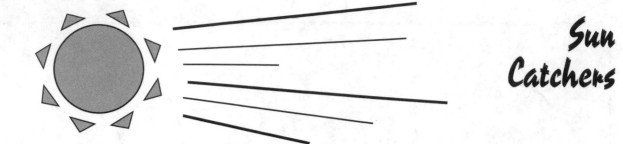

Purpose of the Lesson

to instruct the students in the organization of the elements of art so that the whole composition will be more important than the individual parts

Art History

Marc Chagall (1887–1985) was born in Russia. He never could quite forget the memories of his childhood. His painting "I and the Village" has a dreamlike quality created from jumbled images from folk tales, Jewish proverbs, and memories of his hometown.

Materials

- wax paper
- electric iron
- crayon shavings
- glitter
- 8 ½" x 11" (22 cm x 28 cm) construction paper

- assortment of small and medium-sized leaves
- paste or glue
- scissors

Variations

- old magazines

Procedure

Have each student cut out a frame with one-inch (2.54 cm) borders from a sheet of construction paper. Then have each student cut two 8 ½" x 11" (22 cm x 28 cm) pieces of wax paper.

Tell the students to make a pleasing arrangement of fall leaves of varying sizes, textures, and colors on one of their pieces of wax paper. The arrangements should then be sprinkled with colored crayon shavings and glitter. Have the students lay their other pieces of wax paper on top of their arrangements and iron these with a warm iron. When the wax paper is sealed, ¼"

(.64 cm) should be trimmed from the four sides. The students can finish their creations by pasting them into the construction paper frames and attaching strings for hanging in a sunny window.

Assignment Choices

1. Cut leaves, flowers, ferns, and other plant shapes from construction paper. Lay the shapes on wax paper. Sprinkle them with crayon shavings and place another piece of wax paper over the arrangement. Press with a warm iron and frame the design with a construction paper frame.

2. Cut small geometric shapes from colored construction paper. Arrange the shapes in a kaleidoscopic pattern on a piece of wax paper. Sprinkle with crayon shavings and place another piece of wax paper over the arrangement. Press with a warm iron and frame the design with a construction paper frame.

3. Cut colorful shapes from tissue paper. Make an overlapping design. Sprinkle with crayon shavings and place another piece of wax paper over the design. Iron with a warm iron and frame it with a construction paper frame.

4. Choose a theme, such as sports. Cut out pictures from magazines relating to the theme and arrange the pictures on a piece of wax paper. Sprinkle with crayon shavings and place another piece of wax paper over the arrangement. Iron with a warm iron and frame it with a construction paper frame.

Connection

Marc Chagall's painting, with its many interesting elements, works as a whole to impart long ago memories in a dreamlike sequence.

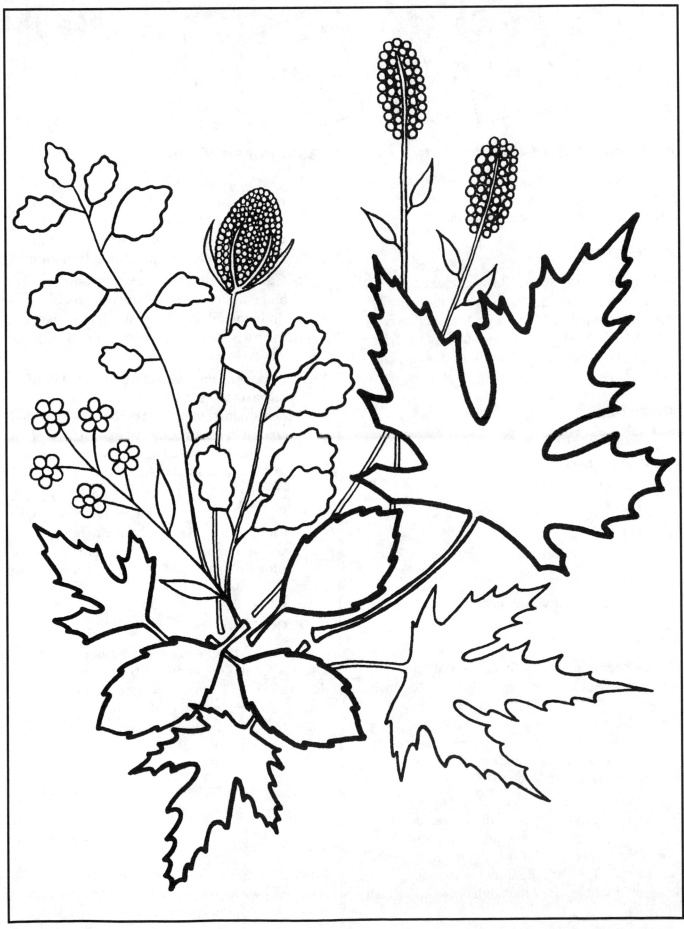

Mag Pix

Purpose of the Lesson

to show that every picture has a focal point and that the background of the picture should be designed to enhance the focal point

Art History

Edouard Manet (1832–1883) was a French painter whose technique may be described as large patches of flat color with few shadows. His painting "The Fifer" was described by his friend Gustave Courbet as being as "flat as a playing card."

Materials

- white construction paper
- old magazines
- scissors
- paste
- pencil
- markers or crayons

Variations

- colored construction paper

Procedure

Before beginning this activity, cut out one interesting picture from old magazines for each student. Cut the pictures no larger than one-fourth the size of an 8 ½" x 11" (22 cm x 28 cm) sheet of construction paper. Paste each picture onto a separate piece of white paper and pass them out to the students.

Challenge the students to fill their pages with drawings which incorporate the magazine pictures and make finished art compositions. Stress the importance of making the magazine picture blend in with the drawing to make an integrated whole. Ask the students to color their drawings.

Assignment Choices

1. Tear up pieces of construction paper to make a fruit bowl filled with fruit. Choose fruits of many colors. Paste the paper pieces onto a piece of construction paper. Draw and color an interesting background.

2. Create and draw your own imaginary animal or cut out pictures of parts of different animals from magazines and paste the parts together to form your own unique animal.

3. Cut out an animal picture from a wildlife magazine. Paste the picture onto a construction paper background. Draw and color a habitat for the animal. Try to show an animal that uses its protective coloring to blend into the landscape.

4. Cut out an animal picture from a magazine. Paste the picture onto a construction paper background. Think about where the animal might be: . . . in the yard? up a tree? sitting on a post? Draw an environment for your animal.

Connection

In Edouard Manet's picture, we can easily see that his focal point is on the fifer's upper body. His background, almost flat gray, helps center attention on the action of the figure. Every art piece (except patterned or positive/negative pieces) should have a focal point.

OSCAR

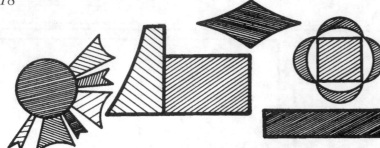

Purpose of the Lesson

to show that a picture is enhanced by the repetition of forms and to give a definite rhythm to a composition

Art History

Paul Cézanne (1839–1906), a painter from the south of France, painted many still-life subjects with overlapping forms. His paintings have a transparent quality. "Fruit Bowl, Glass, and Apples" demonstrates his overlapping technique.

Materials

- paper and pencil for planning
- paste or glue
- black 8 ½" x 11" (22 cm x 28 cm) construction paper
- colored scraps of tissue paper
- scissors
- glitter glue
- clear, glossy spray (optional)

Variations

- string
- coat hanger

Procedure

Have the students plan their stained glass window designs of simple forms on white paper. The forms should be cut out carefully. The practice paper should have large open areas and smaller areas of negative space.

The cutout areas on this paper can be traced onto black construction paper and then the forms can be cut out.

Have the students glue brightly colored tissue paper behind the cutout forms on the black paper. They may also add glitter glue to the negative

spaces, repeating the forms of their main compositions.

Assignment Choices

1. Cut out two identical shapes from black construction paper. Carefully cut out the centers of the shapes, leaving ½" (1.3 cm) borders. Paste tissue paper in between the shapes and attach a string for hanging. Make several more different shapes and use more than one color of tissue paper. Tie the shapes onto a coat hanger to make a mobile.

2. Outline a seasonal silhouette (a Christmas tree, an Easter bunny, etc.) on black construction paper. Cut out the shape and then cut out the center of the shape, leaving ½" (1.3 cm) borders. Paste colored tissue paper behind the open spaces. Hang your design in a sunny window.

3. Cut out circles, squares, and other shapes from black construction paper. Cut out the centers of the shapes, leaving ½" (1.3 cm) borders. Paste tissue paper behind the shapes. When they are dry, arrange and glue the shapes in a composition (abstract or realistic) on white or light colored construction paper.

Connection

As the students study the overlapping technique of Paul Cézanne, they can easily draw complete forms and erase the parts of the forms that overlap.

Lots of Polka Dots

Purpose of the Lesson

to demonstrate the use of symmetrical and asymmetrical balance within the picture plane through the use of the dot technique

Art History

Georges Pierre Seurat (1860–1891), a French artist, liked to paint with small dots of color. This technique known as Pointillism helped him achieve a delicacy of tone and many subtle nuances of color. A good example of Seurat's work is "Le Cirque," or The Circus.

Materials

- tempera paints (or markers)
- toothpicks or cotton swabs
- paint palette (or egg carton)
- 9" x 12" (23 cm x 31 cm) white paper
- pencil

Variations

- watercolor paints
- construction paper

Procedure

Tell the students to each draw a picture or design on a piece of white paper. The designs should be filled with dots created by dipping toothpicks or cotton swabs in tempera paint (markers may be substituted). The dots need to be placed very close together for the right effect. Tell the students to look at their pictures from a distance from time to time. This will help them make sure that there are enough dots to make their pictures effective.

Use this lesson as an opportunity to teach about symmetrical and asymmetrical balance. The picture on page 43 demonstrates symmetrical balance. Identical forms on each side of an axis (such as the clown's face) indicate formal balance. Asymmetrical balance is also demonstrated by such things as the forms on either side of the clown's head. The forms, though different, balance each other through a sensed equilibrium.

Assignment Choices

1. Sketch a picture on colored construction paper. Fill in the picture with brightly colored dots made with a variety of markers.

2. Sketch a picture on a piece of white construction paper. Fill in the picture with colored dots of watercolor paint. Use cotton swabs to apply the dots. Choose the colors that make your picture the most effective.

3. Sketch a picture on gray or black construction paper. Use crayons to fill in your picture with dots.

Connection

As the students explore Georges Pierre Seurat's dot technique, tell them to try different combinations of colors and decide which ones are the most effective for their paintings.

Scratch a Batch of Art

Purpose of the Lesson

to show how the elements of unity, harmony, and variety work together to make an attractive composition

Art History

Georgia O'Keeffe (1887–1986) was a native of Wisconsin. When she was 13 years old, she decided to be an artist. She loved to paint flowers and sun-bleached desert bones. Her painting "White Trumpet Flower" is oversized, and its colors and shading are strong and bold.

Materials

- construction paper
- white tempera paint
- paintbrush
- crayons
- pencil
- scissors
- clear, glossy spray
- nail file, scissors, or other scratching tool

Variations

- India ink
- colored pencils
- dish soap or glycerin

Procedure

To demonstrate the following process, you may wish to use the picture on page 45.

Tell the students that first they will need to draw a design on a piece of white construction paper, using large, abstract shapes. The pictures need to be heavily colored with bright crayons so that none of the white construction paper shows through.

Using a black crayon, the students will then completely cover their designs so that the colors are not showing. They should then use a scratching tool to draw designs or pictures in the black crayon. The crayon colors used under the black should show through when the pictures are scratched.

When the students have finished the scratching step, they may brush in accents with white tempera paint. Finally, spray the finished art pieces with clear gloss.

Assignment Choices

1. Heavily color a sheet of paper with white crayon. Paint over the crayon with India ink. Scratch a picture into the ink and spray the finished product with clear gloss.

2. Fill a piece of paper with colored shapes, using colored pencils. Color over the shapes with a black or violet crayon. Scratch a picture into the crayon and spray the finished product with clear gloss.

3. Color a piece of construction paper with a rainbow of bright crayon colors. Paint over this with white tempera paint. (Add a few drops of dish soap to help the paint adhere to the crayoned areas.) Wait for the paint to dry and then scratch a picture into it. Have an adult spray the finished product with clear gloss.

Connection

As the students scratch their pictures in this project, they can leave dark areas for shading to give a three-dimensional effect, just as Georgia O'Keeffe did.

Purpose of the Lesson

to show the relationship of figure to ground and to demonstrate a simple printing process

Art History

Piet Mondrian (1872–1944), a Dutch painter, developed his own style which he called Neoplasticism. He used only the primary colors, red, blue, and yellow, and the neutrals, white and black. He also used only straight vertical and horizontal lines, as seen in his composition "Red, Blue, and Yellow."

Materials

- construction paper
- paste or glue
- typing or light construction paper
- crayons
- yarn
- scissors

Variations

- various textures for rubbings
- heavy duty foil
- cardboard
- wide paintbrush
- tempera paint
- markers

Procedure

Ask the students to research Native American designs and art. Allow them to choose a design that they find in their research or use the patterns on page 47 for this project. (If they are using the patterns, make sure that they follow the direction notes.)

Have the students color in the patterns, using bright and dark crayons. The patterns should be cut out carefully to preserve the geometric patterns. They may then be pasted onto construction paper and left to dry. When the designs are fully dry, the students will place sheets of typing paper or light construction paper over their entire designs.

Using crayons, they will then color over the entire paper to make crayon rubbings. Instruct the students to then cut out the rubbings, leaving a border around each one, and glue these to a piece of construction paper. Yarn can be attached to both the original art piece and its rubbing counterpart so that both pieces in this project can be used as wall hangings.

Assignment Choices

1. Make your own Indian design, using interesting shapes (birds, arrows, etc.). Paste smaller shapes within the larger shapes and then paste the shapes onto a sheet of construction paper. Decorate the rest of the paper with thunderbirds and other designs cut from foil.

2. Cut Indian motifs out of scrap paper and paste them onto a cardboard background. Let dry. With a wide paintbrush quickly paint over the composition with tempera paint. Place a sheet of construction paper on top of the wet paint and rub firmly to print. Mount the print on a piece of construction paper.

3. Make rubbings of interesting textures on white paper with crayons. Cut out the rubbings in Indian-style geometric shapes and arrange them on a piece of construction paper. Paste down the rubbings. Add marker designs to unify the picture.

Connection

Have students study geometric shapes through the works of Piet Mondrian.

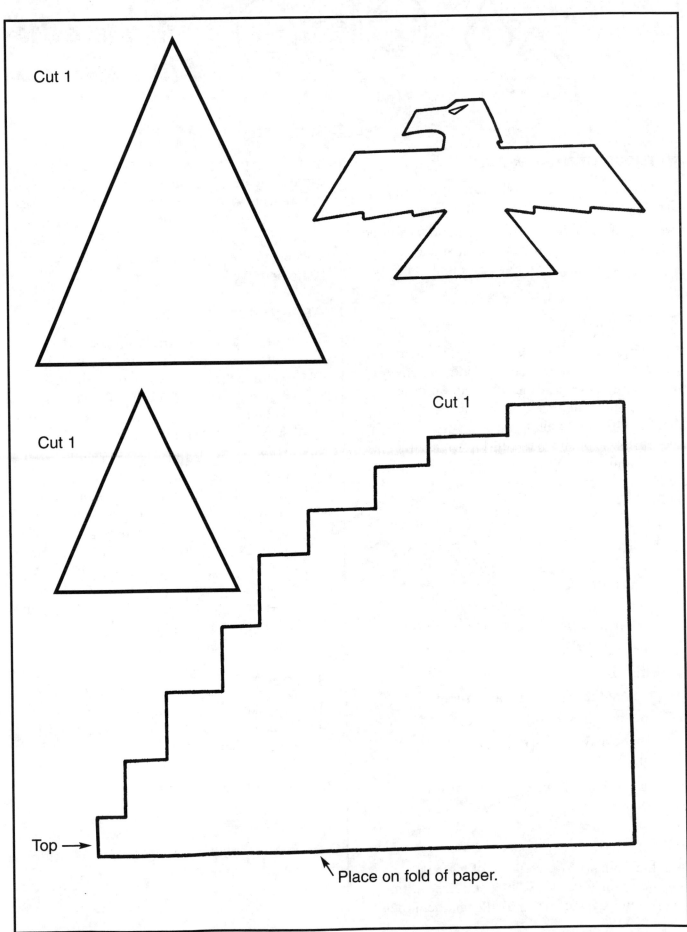

Cut 1

Cut 1

Cut 1

Top →

Place on fold of paper.

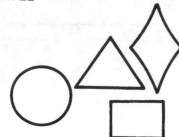

Design a No-Picture Picture

Purpose of the Lesson

to explain the concept of abstract art and to give the students experience in creating it

Note to the Teacher: It is very important for the students to understand that reason and a clear idea of the finished work are essential to creating abstract art.

Art History

Helen Frankenthaler (1928–   ) is an American painter who was born in New York. Helen painted on the floor, using thinned, oil-base paints on untreated canvas. She made colorful patches, drips, organic lines, and swirls. "Before the Caves" is one of her well-known abstract expressionist paintings.

Materials

- scissors
- ruler
- eraser
- bowl of water
- watercolor or tempera paints
- paper towels
- 9" x 12" (23 cm x 31 cm) construction paper
- paste
- pencil
- paintbrushes

Variations

- colored construction paper scraps
- old magazines
- matte and gloss acrylic spray
- shallow tray of clear water
- 12" x 18" (31 cm x 46 cm) construction paper

Procedure

Ask the students to each think of a type of weather: rainstorm, snow, blizzard, ice storm, fog, sunny day, etc. Then challenge them to use abstract shapes to create compositions which capture the moods of their chosen weather. Ask the students to write their titles on the backs of their pictures. When everyone has finished, show the compositions randomly and ask the students to guess what kinds of weather are being portrayed.

Assignment Choices

1. Cut geometric shapes from colored construction paper and magazine scraps. Arrange the shapes on paper until the design is pleasing. (Try different arrangements.) Paste the pieces in place. Spray lightly with matte spray.

2. Think of an idea that you can show in shapes and colors (for example, speed, explosion, drifting, flying, dancing, floating). Cut colors from old magazines and snip them into interesting shapes to make a composition. Glue them to a piece of 9" x 12" (23 cm x 31 cm) white construction paper but leave a 2–3 inch (5–8 cm) border around the design. Spray the finished product lightly with glossy acrylic finish.

Connection

Helen Frankenthaler planned her paintings even though they may seem random and unplanned. When making abstract art, the lessons learned about the color wheel, line, and space, as well as having a basic plan, will help make meaningful art pieces.

Mosaic Mania

Purpose of the Lesson

to learn to use the mosaic technique to create a composition and to understand the use of subtle gradations of color and light in the placement of tesserae

Art History

Joyce Kozloff (1942–   ) was born in New Jersey. She was inspired by Mayan art in the ancient temples of Mexico, Moroccan tile work, American quilts, and arts of other countries. She used painted ceramic tiles and mosaic techniques to design large compositions, such as "The Standard Railroad of the World."

Materials

- 220 grit sandpaper
- scissors
- pencil
- glue
- markers
- 12" x 18" (31 cm x 46 cm) black construction paper
- resource books, videos, and pictures showing Mexican tiles

Variations

- empty egg carton
- old, colorful magazines
- resource materials for Roman motifs
- scrap wood
- black paint
- paintbrush
- beads, baking crystals, etc.
- resource materials showing Egyptian artifacts and desert pictures
- gray, tan, black, and white sandpaper or construction paper
- acrylic matte spray

Procedure

Ask the students to create Mexican tile motifs.

Use resource materials to give them ideas for their designs. Have them draw their designs (such as the one on page 51) on black construction paper. Tell the students to cut sandpaper into 1/4" (.64 cm) squares. These squares should then be pasted onto their designs so that they are touching but not overlapping. The black lines of the designs should still be showing. When the squares are dry, the students can color them with markers.

Assignment Choices

1. Clip many colors from old magazines. Cut each color into squares and organize the pieces of each color in separate compartments of an egg carton. Draw a design with an ancient Roman motif. Fill in the design with the colored squares and carefully paste them down. When the pieces have dried in place, spray them with a light coating of acrylic matte spray.

2. Paint a piece of scrap wood black. Draw an Indian motif of your choice on the wood. Fill it in with beads, baking crystals, or other textures. When the pieces have dried in place, spray with a matte acrylic spray.

3. Draw a picture of the Egyptian desert (this may include pyramids, sphinxes, or other Egyptian features). Create a mosaic, using only shades of neutrals: grays, tans, blacks, and whites. You may use any textured pieces of your choice for this project.

Connection

Viewing the work of Joyce Kozloff will inspire the students to create tiles and use the mosaic technique.

50

Positive and Negative Design

Purpose of the Lesson

to show that the empty spaces (negative space) on a picture plane must be designed and drawn as carefully as the positive forms

Art History

Victor Vasarely (1908–   ), a Hungarian, has lived in France for most of his life. He liked to paint flat, patterned pictures in black and white, such as his large canvas entitled "Vega."

Materials

- construction paper (colors or neutrals)
- glue
- pencil
- scissors
- ruler
- scrap paper for patterns

Variations

- paper doily
- tempera paint
- compass or paper plate
- string
- black marker

Procedure

Give each student two half sheets of construction paper of two different colors or neutrals. Tell the students to clip their papers on top of each other with paper clips. Instruct them to each draw and cut out one half of a totem pole or other form, using the edges of the papers for the center line. The cuts on the two papers should be identical. Have the students unclip the papers and place their two halves together to make whole figures. These pieces should then be pasted on a contrasting background. This technique can be repeated and other forms added to the picture plane for a total composition.

Assignment Choices

1. Fold a paper doily in half. A 6"–7" (15 cm–18 cm) doily is a good size to use. Paint half of the doily black. Leave the other half white. On a piece of 8 ½" x 11" (22 cm x 28 cm) white construction paper, draw a center line the length of the paper. Cut a black strip of construction paper 4 ¼" x 11" (11 cm x 28 cm) and paste it lengthwise on the white paper. Paste the white half of the doily on the black strip of paper, matching the straight edges. Paste the black half of the doily on the white section, matching the straight edges. Use scraps of construction paper to design a medallion to paste in the center of the doily. Attach a string to hang your art project.

2. Fold in half lengthwise a 9" x 12" (23 cm x 31 cm) piece of white construction paper. Draw a picture or use a pattern to make a design. With tempera paint, paint one side of the form red and paint the other half blue. When the paint is dry, place other forms on the picture, reversing the two colors.

Connection

When working with positive/negative art as Victor Vasarely did, the results will essentially be patterned, two-dimensional designs.

Purpose of the Lesson

to explore a variety of printing techniques

Art History

Hokusai (1760–1849) was born in Japan and became interested in art at an early age, especially printing processes. He once made a picture so huge that people could see it only from the tops of houses. Later, he painted two little birds on a grain of rice. His woodcut print entitled "The Great Wave" is very famous.

Materials

- pencil
- scissors
- cardboard from packing boxes
- water-based printing ink or tempera paint and a water cup
- inking pad (glass from a picture frame may be used)
- brayer or paintbrush
- 9" x 12" (23 cm x 31 cm) white drawing paper
- newspapers and paper towels for cleanup
- ruler
- paste or glue

Variations

- art gel
- black fine-point pen or marker
- colored tissue paper
- small objects such as empty thread spools, plastic bottle caps or corks, sandpaper shapes, or other interesting textures
- construction paper scraps

Procedure

Ask the students to each cut a 9" x 12" (23 cm x 31 cm) rectangle from a corrugated packing box and lay it aside. Have the students sketch their simple design ideas onto white paper. From their sketches they should cut out paper patterns for their prints. The patterns can be traced onto cardboard, and the shapes can be cut out and glued to their rectangular pieces of cardboard. Let the glue dry.

Pour some printing ink on the inking pad. Have the students roll out the ink with brayers and apply it to the raised parts of their cardboard designs. The inked side of the cardboard should be carefully applied to a piece of drawing paper and rubbed thoroughly with a ruler or a hand. Tell the students to gently lift their cardboard to see if all of the parts of their designs were printed. If not, they should re-ink their designs and try again until their prints transfer completely. (Tempera paint and brushes may be substituted for brayers and ink.)

Note to the Teacher: Students should wear aprons to protect their clothes.

Assignment Choices

Cut out shapes from colored tissue paper and arrange them on white 9" x 12" (23 cm x 31 cm) drawing paper to make an attractive, abstract design. Remove the shapes and brush over the area with art gel. Arrange the shapes again on top of the gel area. Brush over the tops of the shapes with more gel. Pull the tissue pieces up quickly and lay them aside. Color from the tissue paper will remain on the white paper. When your project has dried, accent it with a fine-point pen or marker.

Connection

Hokusai lived to be 89 years old, and he never stopped trying to become more skilled in printing processes. Students should not be discouraged if their printing processes have to be repeated many times in order to get good prints.

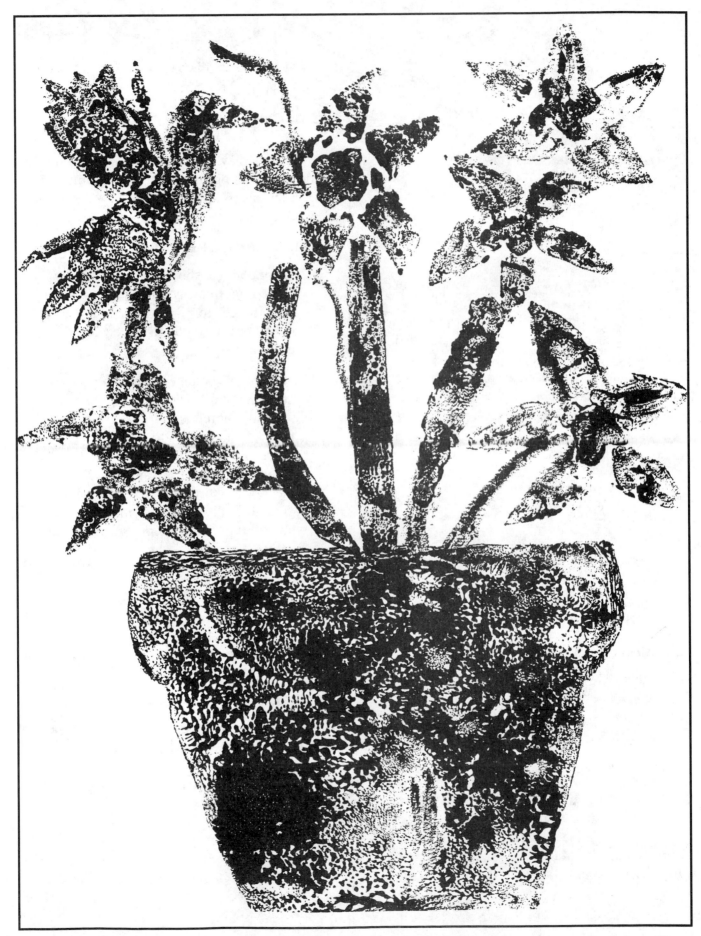

Kite Flight

Purpose of the Lesson

to learn how to use collage effectively and how to show movement in a picture

Art History

Pablo Ruiz Picasso (1881–1973) was born in Spain, but he spent most of his life in France. Picasso liked to invent new ways of presenting reality. He incorporated everyday materials into his paintings, as in "Still Life with Chair Caning" into which he incorporated paint, paper, canvas, and oilcloth and then used rope for a frame.

Materials

- construction paper
- paste or glue
- scissors
- string
- crayons
- pieces of curling ribbon
- old magazines

Variations

- soap flakes
- thread

Procedure

Cut pictures from old magazines to create a composition showing movement. A windy day is a good time for this project. Have the students each cut out a diamond-shaped kite and attach it to a paper hinge (see page 57) to make it pop out from the background. Next, the kite should be glued by its hinge to a background piece of paper.

The students may wish to dress up their kites by coloring, attaching strings, and tying small bits of curling ribbon to the strings.

Assignment Choices

1. Using collage, show the movement of traffic on a freeway or cars on a racetrack. Make hinges to give the cars, road signs, and other items a three-dimensional appearance.

2. Draw or use collage to show a street scene on a rainy day. Cut out and glue many colorful umbrellas to a background piece of paper. Make hinges to glue on the backs of various items to give them a three-dimensional effect. Draw thin, slanting lines (or dip thread in clear glue and arrange small pieces of it in a slanted direction) to show the movement of rain.

3. Draw or use collage to show a favorite winter sport (skiing, ice skating, snowmobiling, etc.). Make hinges to glue to the backs of the athletes to make them pop out from the background. Glue soap flakes on the composition to simulate snow.

Connection

Pablo Picasso is a fine example of how important it is for artists to keep an open and inventive mind when creating art. The students should try to devise new ideas, shades of color, and ways of presenting art.

Glue this end to the tab.

FOLD

FOLD

TAB

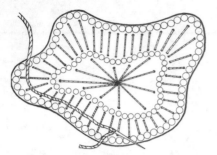

Wriggle into Weaving

Purpose of the Lesson

to use a variety of materials to create artistic weavings and to sharpen concentration and motor skills

Art History

Jean Lurcat (1892–1966), a French painter and designer, became interested in weaving and made many decorative and colorful tapestries with modern flair.

Materials

- construction paper (red and green)
- construction paper scraps
- pieces of ribbon, yarn, cord, etc.

- paste
- scissors
- compass with pencil
- tape

Variations

- plastic straws
- stapler and staples
- old ribbon and beads
- glue

- ¹/₄" and ³/₄" (.6 cm and 1.9 cm) colored sequins
- scrap yarn and darning needles
- tagboard

Procedure

Ask the students to each draw a circle 8" (20 cm) in diameter circle on a piece of red construction paper. They should each then draw a freehand swirl starting in the center (see page 59). There should be about seven layers to the swirls with about ¹/₂" (1.3 cm) between each layer. The last layer will run off the edge of the circle, so it will need to be taped to keep the circle closed.

Next, have the students cut 10" (25.4 cm) strips of construction paper in random widths and colors. They may also cut pieces of cord, yarn, or ribbon to the same length. Help the students weave the paper pieces through their circles until they are completely filled. Strings and ribbons can then be woven on top of the paper pieces. Have the students trim off the ends so that they are even with the circle. The finished woven circles can be mounted on dark green construction paper.

Assignment Choices

1. Arrange four straws into a star shape and staple them together with two staples. Using ribbons of various kinds and colors, weave in and out of the straw formation. Leave about the last 2" (5 cm) of the straws unwoven and securely tie off the ribbon. Attach a loop of ribbon to the back of the weaving to use as a hanger.

   Glue beads to the center of the star to cover up the staples. Glue a bead to the end of each straw for decoration. Use and enjoy the weaving as a unique wall hanging.

2. Cut a random shape from a piece of tagboard. With the point of a compass, punch holes in the shape in a similar fashion to the diagram on the bottom of page 59. Stitch thin yarn through the punched holes. Then use thicker yarn to weave through the stitches. Attach a loop of yarn to the back of the weaving to use as a hanger. Paste small sequins around the center design and outside edge. Attach three pieces of thin yarn to the bottom of the hanging and add three large sequins to the ends of the strings.

Connection

From the example of Jean Lurcat, the students should learn that there are many weaving stitches and many interesting fabrics that make weavings truly distinctive.

58

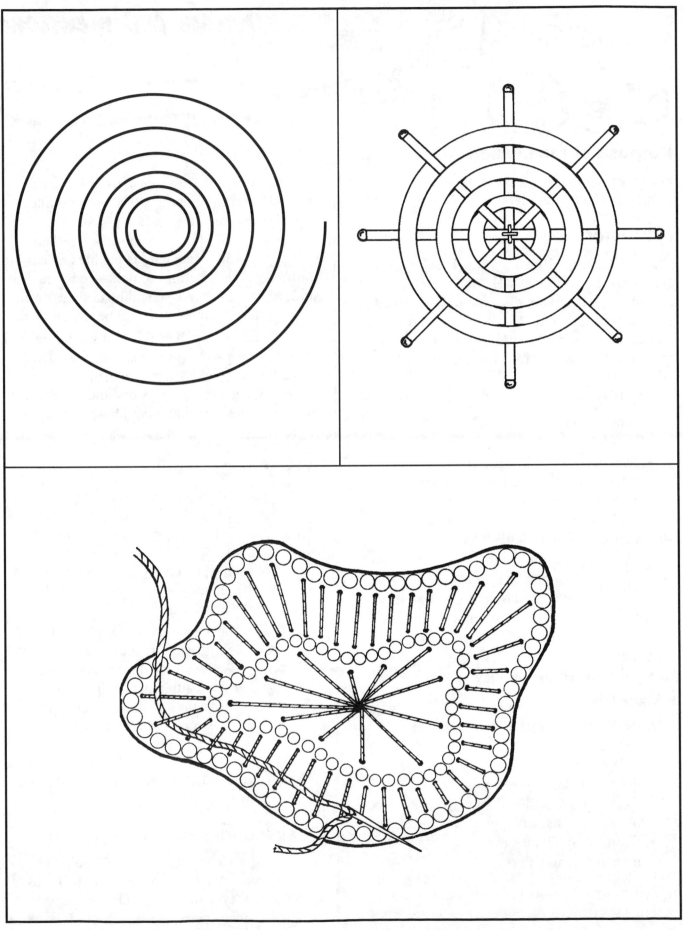

Dynamic Dimensions

Purpose of the Lesson

to experience designing three-dimensional art using recyclable materials

Art History

Claes Oldenburg (1929–   ) was born in Sweden and grew up in America. He liked to make sculptures of everyday objects in plaster, steel, and aluminum. He took soft objects and transformed them into hard metal, as in his steel and aluminum sculpture "Geometric Mouse."

Materials

- scrap paper
- pencil
- telephone wire (Scrap cable wire can usually be obtained from telephone companies free of charge. Split open the gray sheath and take out the thin, colored wires inside ahead of time.)
- plastic bucket and water
- long-handled plastic spoon
- box of plaster or plaster strips (Use fresh plaster. Old plaster does not set up properly. Keep dry until ready to use.)
- newspaper to cover work surface
- paper towels for cleaning up

Variations

- cardboard from packing cartons
- toothpicks
- glue
- brightly colored spray paint
- metal scraps (nails, screws, washers, nuts, old keys, bolts, small pieces of metal, etc.)
- liquid welding adhesive
- metallic spray paint

Procedure

Ask the students to draw designs or pictures suitable for wire sculptures (such as buildings, animals, or human figures). Pass out the colored wires so that the students can construct their sculptures. Telephone wire is pliable and easy to form into a composition. Emphasize to the students that the wires should be arranged well and that their sculptures should be sturdily built.

Let the students dip their finished sculptures into wet plaster (or wrap the wires if they are using plaster strips), making sure all of the wires are coated. When the plaster is dry, the sculptures may be mounted on cardboard bases and/or painted.

Assignment Choices

1. Create a toothpick sculpture. Make a sketch of the finished sculpture before you begin. Cut out a cardboard base for your sculpture. Spray-paint the base and the sculpture separately in a bright color. Finally, mount your sculpture on the cardboard base.

2. Gather together some metal pieces such as nails, screws, washers, nuts, old keys, and bolts. Use liquid welding to assemble them together in an attractive composition. When your sculpture is thoroughly dry, glue it to a strong base; two layers of cardboard pasted together or a piece of scrap wood will work well. When the glue has dried, spray the sculpture and its base with metallic paint.

Connection

The works of Claes Oldenburg will help the students understand that the material being used dictates what type of form can be developed. A childlike essence permeates much of his work.

Name Game

Purpose of the Lesson

to show the importance of organizing the total picture plane into an attractive and dynamic finished product

Art History

Henri de Toulouse-Lautrec (1864–1901) was born in France. He became a master of poster art. People liked his posters so much that they were often taken down from walls or theater marquees as soon as they were put up.

Materials

- construction paper 12" x 18" (31 cm x 46 cm)
- large construction paper scraps, various colors
- scissors
- pencil
- paste or glue
- pre-cut paper squares
- a book or chart showing various styles of print
- old magazines and newspapers
- markers, pens, paints and brushes, or crayons

Procedure

Before beginning this lesson, cut out squares of white scrap paper in a uniform size. Give each student enough squares to represent every letter in his or her name. Help the students make patterns for the letters of their names. Each letter should be the height of the block with no vertical space left over.

When the students have made acceptable letter patterns, ask them to choose colors of construction paper for the letters of their names. Using the patterns, the students should then trace and cut out the letters and paste them onto construction paper backgrounds. Finally, they may decorate their letters and/or backgrounds with shapes or pictures (from magazines, newspapers, or drawings) of things that reveal something about their personal interests.

Assignment Choices

1. Choose a topic word for a picture (plants, frogs, art materials, science, geography, etc.). Cut out letters from magazines to form the chosen topic word. Draw an attractive composition to illustrate the selected word.

2. Cut out letters from magazines to make a short slogan such as "Wish on a star" or "Have a great day." Then find and cut out pictures to illustrate the slogan. Arrange the slogan and pictures in an attractive way and paste them onto brightly colored construction paper. Add details with pens, markers, or paints.

3. Cut out some interesting letters from newspapers or magazines. Make a composition out of these letters by gluing them onto a construction paper background. Unify the composition with marker drawings or words.

Connection

As the students work on their posters, they should notice some of Henri de Toulouse-Lautrec's methods in the placement of lettering and the use of bright colors.

Seed-sational Creations

Purpose of the Lesson

to create three-dimensional projects which portray nature, using natural textures

Art History

John Love (1850–1880) was born in Indiana. Love was the first professional Indiana artist to paint outdoors. James Whitcomb Riley wrote a poem to honor him. Love's painting "The Sycamores" gives one the feeling of walking in the woods.

Materials

- 9" x 12" or 12" x 18" (23 cm x 31 cm or 31 cm x 46 cm) piece of cardboard or ¹⁄₄" (.64 cm) plywood
- acrylic paint
- navy beans, rice, mixed beans, birdseed, etc.
- glue
- polymer medium
- permanent markers
- pencil
- bowl of water
- paintbrush
- reference materials

Variations

- miscellaneous seeds, assorted pasta
- pine cones, feathers
- yarn
- tab from soda can
- 9" x 12" (23 cm x 31 cm) colored construction paper
- spray paint (Have an adult use spray paint.)
- hot-glue gun (for teacher's use only)
- large, flat cardboard box

Procedure

Open this activity by discussing and researching the rain forest as a class.

Ask the students to draw their own rain forest scenes on pieces of cardboard or wood. (See the example on page 65.) They should include some of the plants and animals that they learned about in the first part of this activity. Tell the students to then fill in the plants and animals with a mixture of seeds and to color the sky and ground with markers or acrylic paints. The beans and seeds offer a variety of natural colors; however, they may be colored with permanent markers after they have been glued to the cardboard. When the pictures have completely dried, paint several coats of a polymer medium over them to fix the seeds and beans on permanently.

Assignment Choices

1. Draw a picture of an owl on a piece of cardboard. Cut it out. Glue seeds and pieces of pine cones on the head and body. Add feathers for the wings and tail. Make a hanger from the tab of a soft can. Ask an adult to glue it on to the back of your composition with a hot-glue gun.

2. Collect seed pods, weeds, leaves, and flowers that are dried or fresh. Arrange them on a piece of colored construction paper. Ask an adult to carefully place your picture in a large, flat cardboard box and spray it with the paint color of your choice. Remove the picture when it dries.

Connection

John Love used nature to create his art. The students will also use nature as their inspiration in this activity.

Weather Art

Purpose of the Lesson

to create multifaceted compositions (These pictures will exemplify movement, weather, time, and texture.)

Art History

El Greco (1541–1614) was born Domenikos Theotokopoulos on the island of Crete, which is off the coast of Greece. He spent most of his life in Spain where he was given the nickname El Greco. He painted a gathering storm over the Spanish city of Toledo in "View of Toledo."

Materials

- 9" x 12" (239 cm x 31 cm) smoky blue construction paper
- pencil
- glue
- silver glitter
- white fluorescent paint
- tempera paints
- paintbrush
- a book about stars
- a black marker or black paint
- a ruler

Variations

- 9" x 12" (23 cm x 31 cm) white construction paper
- red, green, yellow, and clear baking crystals
- cotton balls
- white sand
- sifter
- food coloring
- compass

Procedure

Have the students create moonlit pictures which include silhouetted figures and trees, the moon and stars, and water reflecting the moonlight. To give the moon its shining effect, the students may use white fluorescent paint which has been slightly toned down with a little tempera paint and water. The silhouettes may be drawn or painted in, and the water may be cut out of smoky-blue construction paper. Accents may be added to the water, using glue and glitter. Help the students research star constellations and tell them to lightly mark two or three star constellations on their pictures. Tell them to apply a tiny dot of glue to each dot with a toothpick. (Do not use glue bottles to apply the glue.) Sprinkle silver glitter over the glue to make stars.

Assignment Choices

1. Draw a windy, springtime scene. Glue green baking crystals on the trees to simulate new leaves. Use red and yellow baking crystals as petals for flowers. Use a thin layer of cotton for a cloud. Paint umbrellas and clothes in bright colors.

2. Draw an outdoor scene with raindrops and a rainbow. Add trees, puddles, a sun, and clouds, along with some lively people. With tiny dots of paste, add clear baking crystals for the raindrops. Color white sand with food coloring in the colors of the rainbow (red, yellow, blue, orange, green, and violet). Apply paste to one section of the rainbow at a time and sift the colored sand on that part of the arc. Use tempera paints to finish the picture.

3. Draw an autumn scene with leaves falling from the trees. Use orange baking crystals to color the sun, falling leaves, and leaf pile. Color the remaining parts of the picture with tempera paints.

Connection

El Greco's painting "View of Toledo" shows a realistic storm that is almost frightening to look at. El Greco's painting will inspire students to make meaningful compositions.

Presents for Parents

Purpose of the Lesson

to create useful and attractive gifts from simple, everyday materials

Art History

James Whistler (1834–1903) was born in Massachusetts. He painted with a flat technique, using thin washes. He compared his paintings to music, naming them nocturnes and symphonies. His best known work is "Arrangement in Black and Gray: The Artist's Mother."

Parents are very busy people. Here is a very thoughful gift to help Mom or Dad keep things organized.

Materials

- corrugated packing case
- 1 ½" (4 cm) wide cardboard tubing (paper towel, bathroom tissue, or gift wrap tubes)
- ruler
- pencil
- scrap paper
- glue
- scissors
- thick markers
- gummed labels
- contact paper, wallpaper, spray paint (adult use only), or tempera paint

Procedure

The students will be making organizers from a cluster of cardboard tubes. The tubes serve as holding containers for a variety of items. Although the patterns and directions suggest they be used for desk items, such as letter openers, pens, paper clips, rubber bands, scissors, and pencils, students can choose labels that represent other items their parents might store in the tubes (straight pins, safety pins, loose change, etc.)

Assignment

To make a gift organizer, start by cutting out two ovals from thick cardboard for a base. (You may wish to first cut an oval pattern from a piece of scrap paper so that you can be assured of getting a perfect oval shape.) On one of the ovals, draw a center line. Lay the pattern of circles from page 69 on the oval, matching the center lines. Trace and cut out the circles in the formation shown in the pattern. Paste the uncut cardboard oval underneath the oval with the circular cut-outs to assure a strong base.

Cut six tubes to the following lengths:
7 ¼" (18cm) for a letter opener
5 ¾" (15 cm) for scissors
5 ½" (14 cm) for pens
4" (10 cm) for pencils
3" (8 cm) for rubber bands
2" (5 cm) for paper clips

Use the second pattern on page 69 to diagonally trim the tops off of the tubes. Cover the base with contact paper, wallpaper, or paint, but do not cover the cutout area. Cover the tubes, except for their bottom ends. Write on and attach labels to the tubes. Glue the tubes to the base. Parents will certainly be pleased with this new organizer.

Connection

James Whistler's mother must have appreciated the efforts of her son to paint her portrait. The students' mothers and fathers will also appreciate the handmade gifts from this lesson.

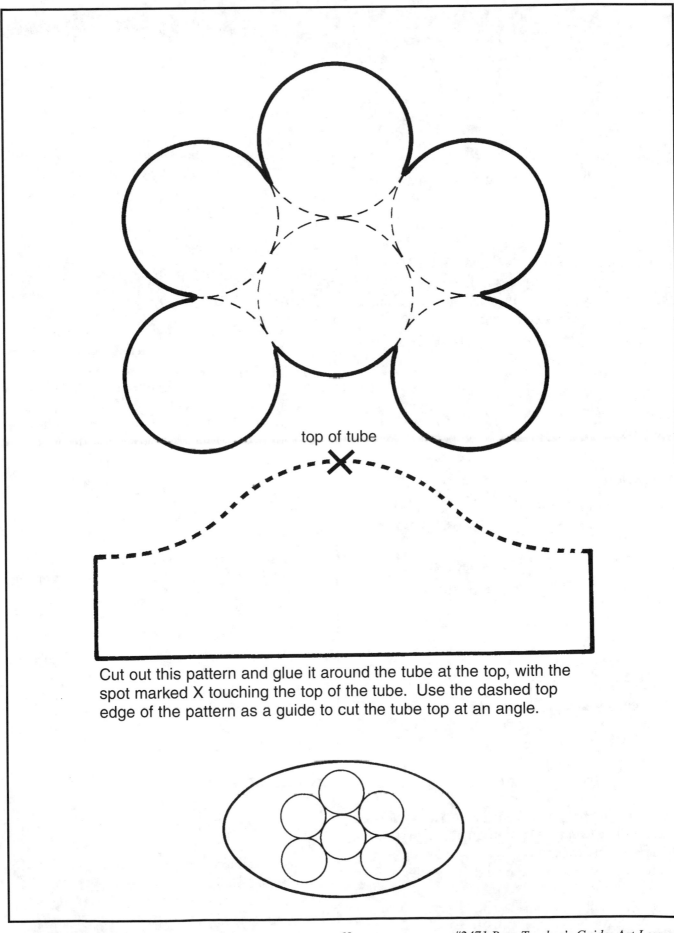

top of tube

Cut out this pattern and glue it around the tube at the top, with the spot marked X touching the top of the tube. Use the dashed top edge of the pattern as a guide to cut the tube top at an angle.

Let's Talk Turkey

Purpose of the Lesson

to create holiday art from recyclable materials

Art History

Pieter Bruegel the Elder (c. 1525–1569) was a talented painter from the Netherlands. Many members of his family were also painters, but his work was particularly outstanding. He liked to paint landscapes and scenes from everyday life, such as "Peasant Wedding Feast."

Materials

- hot-glue gun and glue sticks
- white glue
- brown tissue paper
- construction paper
- art gel paste and a large plastic bowl
- small plastic bowls
- paintbrushes and a bowl of water
- scissors
- funnel
- empty dishwashing soap bottle
- paper punch
- aluminum foil
- goose (or colored) feathers
- newspaper
- plastic garbage bags

Variations

- empty bathroom-tissue tubes
- markers

Procedure

Have each student make a 4" (10 cm) rolled ball of aluminum foil for the body of his or her turkey. Ask the students to cut brown tissue paper into 2" (5 cm) wide strips. Mix the art gel paste in a large plastic bowl according to the directions on the package. If the gel seems too thick, add more water. Pour the mixture into an empty dishwashing soap bottle by using a funnel. Squeeze individual portions of the glue into small plastic bowls for the students.

Tell the students to brush the glue onto their foil balls and then to wrap the balls in brown tissue. This procedure should be repeated until there are four layers on each ball. Place these turkey bodies on a plastic garbage bag and let them dry overnight. Draw and cut out a head and feathers and glue them to the body.

Assignment Choices

1. Cut a 4" (10 cm) cylinder from a bathroom-tissue paper tube. Trace a turkey head from the pattern in the first box on page 71, or make your own out of red construction paper. Add a yellow beak and a paper-punch dot for an eye. Color the cardboard tube brown by using a marker or paint. Cut a slit in one end and insert the turkey's head. To create the feathers, pleat a 3" x 10" (8 cm x 25 cm) piece of brown construction-paper strip and place it inside of the cardboard tube.

2. Make a cone shape for a turkey body by using the pattern in the bottom box on page 71. Cut out the pattern for the head, place it on a folded piece of paper as directed, trace it, and cut it out. Paste the head onto the cone at the point, placing one piece on each side. To make the turkey's tail, cut strips of construction or tissue paper and stuff them into the cone. Secure the tail pieces with paste or glue. Draw or cut and paste wings onto the sides of the turkey.

Connection

Bruegel's "Peasant Wedding Feast" shows many people gathered to enjoy a feast of foods and the company of each other. Studying a painting of such a feast and celebration will create a mood for creating Thanksgiving decorations.

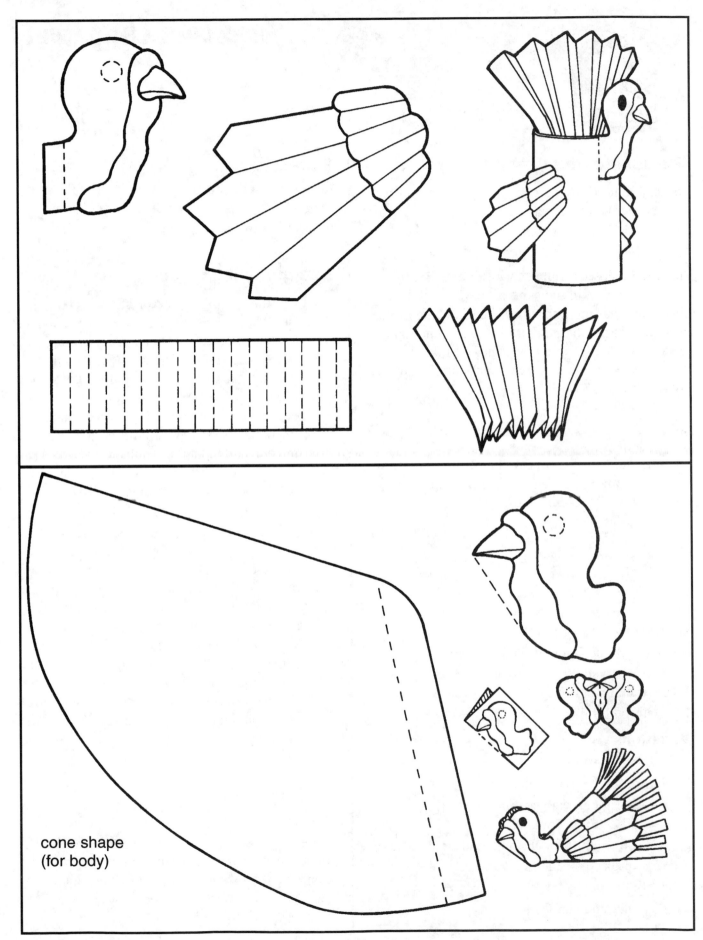

cone shape
(for body)

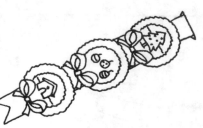

Awesome Ornaments

Purpose of the Lesson

to recycle items that are normally thrown away into attractive Christmas decorations

Art History

Grandma Moses (Anna Mary Roberts, 1860-1961) was born in the state of New York. Her painting "Out for Christmas Trees" is one of her best known paintings. Perhaps it is so popular because of its decorative touches and details. Grandma Moses was a true American primitive, as was her style.

Materials

- frosted or clear plastic lids from butter tubs and other containers (The lids should be about 4" [10 cm] in diameter.)
- clear tape
- scissors
- pencil
- green scrap paper
- white glue
- spray snow or silver glitter
- #30 monofilament fishing line
- craft crystal tri-beads (or any recycled crystal beads or glitter)
- straight pins

Variations

- $1/4$" (.6 cm) red and green sequins
- iridescent pipe cleaners
- red or green velvet ribbon in 1" (2.5 cm) and $1/4$" (.6 cm) widths
- plastic ring from around a gallon milk jug
- old Christmas cards
- glitter
- stapler and staples

Procedure

Give each student three plastic lids and have them use the lids to complete the assignment choices below.

Assignment Choices

1. Cut the rim off of one plastic lid, creating a ring that is approximately $3/8$" (.9 cm) wide. Glue torn pieces of green paper around the ring to resemble a wreath. On the plastic disk left from the lid, trace and cut out two overlapping bells (use the bell pattern on page 73). Glue red and green sequins on the bands of the bells. Around the edges of the bells, glue crystal beads or glitter. Tie the bells to the inside of the rim with fishing line and add a hanger loop.

2. Cut the rims off of three clear or frosted plastic lids. Discard the rims or save them for another project. Form three iridescent pipe cleaners into circles and glue them to the edges of the circles. Place them on a flat surface and tape them down until they are dry. Fold one end of 1" (2.5 cm) wide velvet ribbon over a milk jug ring and staple. Cut a "V" at the end of the ribbon The ribbon should be 24" (61 cm) long. Cut colorful pictures from Christmas cards and paste them to the decorated disks. Add bows from the $1/4$" (.6 cm) wide velvet ribbon. Add glitter if desired. Staple the disks to the long velvet ribbon and use it as a wall hanging.

Connection

Grandma Moses used simple materials to make her paintings. Similarly, the students can use simple materials and careful craftsmanship to make attractive Christmas decorations.

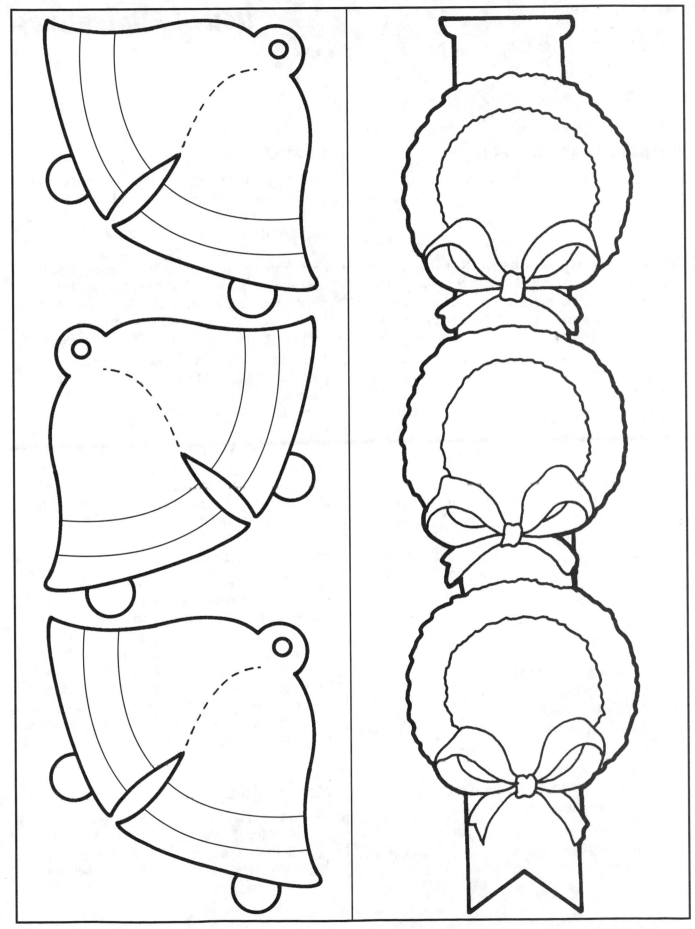

 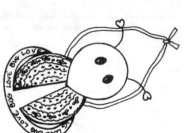 

Voilà! Valentines!

Purpose of the Lesson

to make thoughtful gifts for Valentine's Day

Art History

Robert (Clark) Indiana (1928–) was born in Indiana. This well-known pop artist changed his name from Robert Clark to Robert Indiana. He combines stenciled lettering with areas of bright color. His sculpture "Love" is well-known throughout the country, and it greets visitors at the entrance to the Indianapolis Art Museum.

Materials

- small, white paper plates
- scissors
- glue and/or paste
- white paper doily
- 6" (15 cm) telephone cable wire or light wire
- red-hot candies
- red paint and a paintbrush
- marker
- red curling ribbon
- red construction paper

Variations

- modeling or floral clay
- bottle cap that is ³/₄" (2 cm) in diameter and 1" (2.5 cm) thick
- red, pink, and white construction and tissue paper
- glitter
- cardboard tube from bathroom tissue
- red paper doily
- white paint
- old greeting cards
- tagboard

Procedure

Give each student two small paper plates. One will be used as a bug body, and the bug's head will be cut out of the other. Have them paint the backs of their plates with red paint. When the plates have dried, tell the students to cut out a head from one of them. On the other plate the students should write the words "Love Bug" around the edge of the backside. Using the white side of the body plate, the students can write a simple Valentine message, such as "I love you."

Next, the students should attach wires for antennae to the inside edge of the head. The antennae can be decorated with hearts at the ends. Give two red-hot candies to each student to glue on as eyes.

Finally, help the students make wings for their bugs out of paper doilies. To make the wings stick out, the students can fold over ¹/₄" (.6 cm) allowance on the straight edges and only glue these edges to the plate.

Assignment Choice

To make a fountain of hearts, draw four red, four pink, and four white hearts on the folded edge of paper. Cut out the hearts so that they can open up like little cards. Write a short Valentine message inside each one. Decorate the fronts of the hearts with glitter. Paste 5" (13 cm) of wire to the back of each heart. Fill a bottle cap with clay and arrange the wires in the cap. For a base, cut out a heart shape from a piece of cardboard, paint it red, and glue the bottle cap to the center. Give the fountain to a special person.

Connection

Robert Indiana proves that innovative things can be done with simple materials. As the students explore this lesson, perhaps they, using simple materials, can devise innovations of their own.

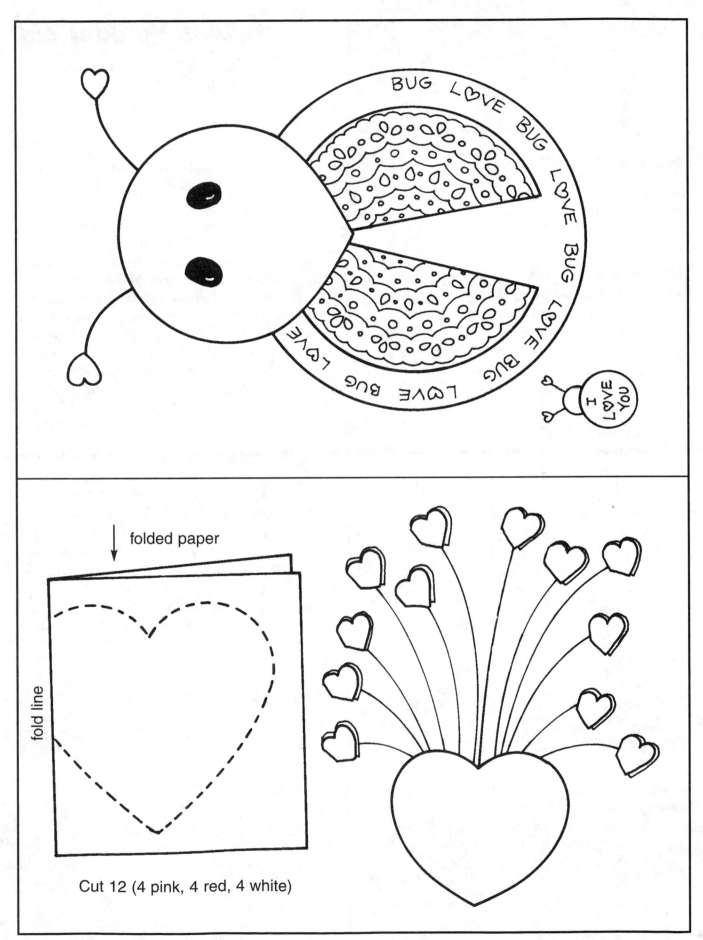

BUG LOVE BUG LOVE BUG

I LOVE YOU

folded paper

fold line

Cut 12 (4 pink, 4 red, 4 white)

Bright Bunnies and Egg-cellent Eggs

Purpose of the Lesson

to use simple materials to explore the ancient art of stained glass construction

Art History

Albrecht Dürer (1471–1528) was a German artist who was skilled in painting and printmaking. He never tired of adding touches to his works in order to make them perfect. We see this patience and attention to meticulous detail in Dürer's watercolor entitled "A Hare."

Materials

- brightly colored tissue paper
- black construction paper
- white glue
- pencil

- scissors
- string
- small hole punch
- ribbon
- parchment or onionskin paper

Variations

- egg-shaped hosiery containers or large, plastic Easter eggs
- polymer medium

- paintbrush
- glitter
- sequins
- beads
- newspaper
- plastic bags

Procedure

Give each student two pieces of black construction paper and have them trace both the inside and outside lines of the pattern on page 77 onto the paper. Instruct them to cut along both lines on both pieces of paper so that they each end up with two black Easter bunny outlines.

Next, have the students trace only the outer line of the same pattern onto parchment or onion paper and cut out the bunny shape. Tell the students to cut out or tear random shapes of tissue paper and glue them onto the parchment or onionskin bunny shape. The tissue should overlap and cover both sides of the paper. Help the students sandwich the bunny shape between the two construction-paper bunny outlines and glue into place. Tell them to trim any excess tissue or parchment paper that may be hanging out of the black outline. Finally, punch a hole at the top of each of their bunnies and insert a ribbon. Hang the Easter bunnies in a sunny window.

Assignment Choice

To begin making a multicolored Easter egg, brush a layer of polymer medium (water-based varnish) onto an egg-shaped hosiery container or large, plastic Easter egg. Cut or tear shapes of tissue paper and place them over the polymer covering. Allow the tissue pieces to overlap. Brush another layer of polymer over the top of the tissue and place it on a plastic garbage bag to dry overnight. Further decorate this colorful egg with bits of ribbon, sequins, beads, or glitter.

Connection

Because Albrecht Dürer was such a perfectionist, his rabbit seems so lifelike, as though it might start hopping at any moment. Teachers should inspire their students to do their best work in every art piece they create.

Art Lesson—Generic Form

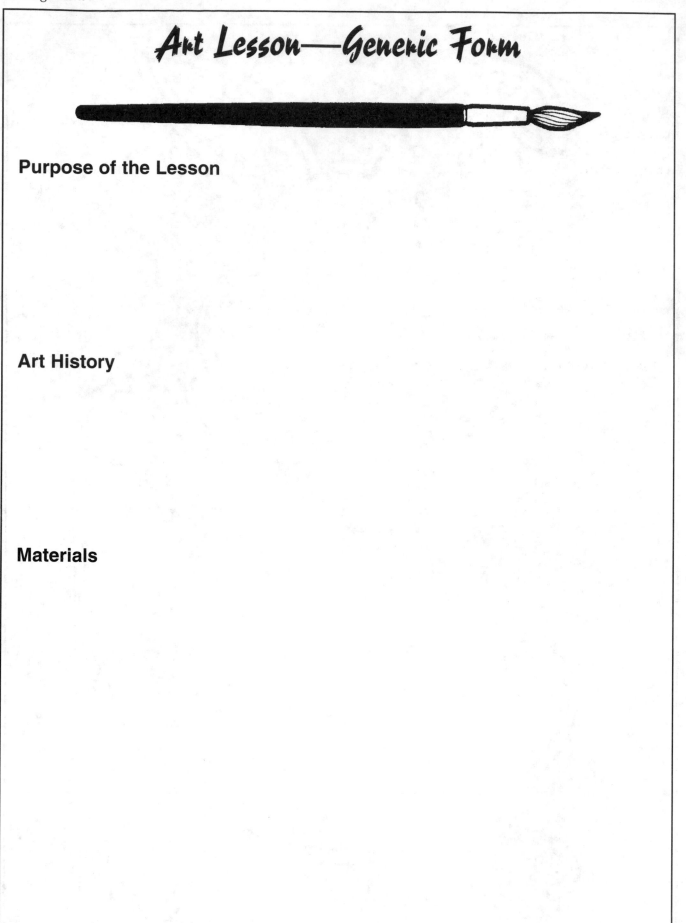

Purpose of the Lesson

Art History

Materials

78

Art Lesson—Generic Form (cont.)

Procedure

Assignment Choices

Connection

Art Sources

Books

Bertilli, Carlo, Ed. *Mosaics.* (Gallery Books, 1988) (*Lesson 11*)

Diamondstein, Barbaralee, Ed. *The Art World: A 75 Year Treasury of Artnews.* (Artnews Books, 1977) (*Lesson 19*)

Fleming, William. *Arts and Ideas.* (Hart, Rinehart, and Winston, 1986) (*Lessons 4, 7, and 28*)

Gombrich, E. H. *The Story of Art* (12th Edition). (Phaedon Press Ltd., 1974) (*Lesson 36*)

Grolier Multimedia Encyclopedia. (1993) (*Lesson 27*)

Heller, Nancy G. *Women Artists.* (Abbeville Press, 1991) (*Lessons 1, 2, 12, 13, 22, 23, 34*)

Herberholz, Barbara. *Art in Action: Enrichment Programs I and II.* (Coronado Publishers, 1987) (*Program I: Lessons 3, 8, 25; Program II: Lessons 14, 20, 31*)

Janson, H. W. and Anthony F. *History of Art.* (Harry N. Abrams, 1986) (*Lessons 5, 6, 10, 15, 16, 17, 18, 21, 29, 32, 33, 35*)

Loria, Stefano. *Masters of Art: Picasso.* (Peter Bedrick Books, 1995) (*Lesson 26*)

Walker, John. *National Gallery of Art.* (Harry N. Abrams, Inc., 1975) (*Lesson 9*)

Web Sites

ARTSEDGE: The National Arts and Education Information Network
http://artsedge.kennedy-center.org/

Chinese Historical and Cultural Project (San Jose, CA)
http://www.dnai.com/rutledge/CHCP_home.html

Mark Kistler's Imagination Station (3-D drawing)
http://www.draw3d.com/index.html